D1453564

THE PELLET STOVE
ALMANACK

Home Heating Joins the 21st Century

BY KEN MACDONALD

WITH ILLUSTRATIONS BY SAM GUAY

For Judith.

Thanks for Everything.

Love Always.

ACKNOWLEDGEMENTS

A big Thank You to everyone who helped shepherd this book along from its inception. To those who reviewed, suggested, and commented on the manuscript as it grew, you folks were vital. Special thanks to Karen Harman-Smeltz, Steve Walker, and Craig Issod; as representatives of the wood and pellet heating industry, I appreciate the time and information you generously donated, and the improvements to the manuscript that resulted. Jonathan Talbot, for your insightful advice on navigating the self-publishing waters. Sam, for all the fun ideas for illustrations. To all those I spoke with about the project and reflected my own enthusiasm back, doubled. And Samantha, for being the cutest cover-cat we could have hoped for.

Special thanks to the best teachers I ever had, my parents, John and Helene MacDonald, who instilled a lifelong desire to learn and understand. Wish you were still here to see this. And thanks to Sierra, Skye, and Zakai who remind me that the generations following us should inform our decisions each day if we want to leave them a better world.

Finally, to my wife, who helped keep me focused on moving the book forward, as well as contributing her editing skills.

You've all helped make this book more than I could have done by myself. Heartfelt thanks to all.

Ken - December 2012

CONTENTS

INTRODUCTION

Wood pellet heating systems are a part of the most rapidly growing segment of America's energy economy. Renewable and sustainably produced bio-fuels are becoming increasingly prominent in transportation, power generation, home and commercial heating. Even the defense sector is using alternative fuels for their ships, planes, and land vehicles. In the future, an appropriate mix of these renewable fuel sources will be increasingly important aspects of economy, environmental protection, and national security management.

Wood pellet stoves are a relatively easy and affordable way for consumers to start utilizing alternative energy sources, and an ideal means toward a more sustainable, comfortable, and economical means of heating their homes and businesses. While there is upfront expense, in many cases, the savings in fuel cost alone can cover the initial investment within two to three years, and yield significant savings in subsequent years. Many homes have suitable locations for a pellet stove, especially those already equipped with an existing wood stove or an under-utilized fireplace. Many other homes can be adapted easily, as the main requirement is a blank spot on the outside wall that can accept a four-inch direct-vent exhaust for the stove. 4" VENT *

Many folks are used to the convenience of "heating with the thermostat", and consider heating with visible flame (as produced by either a wood or a pellet stove) a throwback to the Flintstones.

1

However, modern central heating systems have struck a deal with the devil; they are a compromise between a somewhat comfortable living space with the convenience of just throwing money at the problem. Even though the fuel for a pellet stove is pretty low-tech—after all, we are talking about burning sawdust here—the other technologies embedded in the pellet stove allow it to create a sense of comfort in our homes equal to or exceeding any other currently available type of heating system. In fact, the wood pellet stove is one of the only heating systems available that truly has a 21st-century design – most heating appliances for the home rely on a technology perfected when Chester Alan Arthur was President.

With the advent of the modern pellet stove, many of us have realized the dream of living in a far more comfortable home, hand-in-hand with extraordinary savings, not to mention the benefit to your local economy and the environment. However, heating with pellets is not for everybody; unlike heating with oil, gas, or electricity, it requires more personal involvement than watching someone stroll across your lawn with a big hose, and writing a big check to the heating oil company each month. Some homes are not suitable for a pellet stove installation either. Their internal room layout, or the limits imposed by the surrounding community, can be serious obstacles to successfully incorporating one of these appliances. As the stove owner is required to physically move the pellets around, that's not for everyone either. Hence, it's important to understand these potential drawbacks before investing your time, energy, and dollars.

After talking with dozens of folks, it seems that pellet stoves are widely misunderstood, by not only prospective consumers but even by some of the dealers selling them. While many retailers I've spoken to are nice and know the spec sheets on their products inside and out, only a few can properly evaluate whether the stoves will integrate well with a specific home layout, existing heating system, and lifestyle. The purpose of this guide is to give you the necessary tools and understanding to get to the heart of these matters for yourself.

WHY WE'RE HERE

I chose to write this introduction to wood pellet stoves since there was very little practical information available when we took the plunge and bought ours a couple of years ago. This information was not readily found on the Internet, no in-depth books were sold at Amazon—except for an interesting looking one (unfortunately priced at well north of $100) that covered everything from consumer use to building a hundred megawatt generating station. Even the salespeople at some of the local dealers couldn't do much more than parrot the specifications and BTU figures out of the glossy brochures. A couple of heating seasons later, sadly the situation is much the same. Although the relevant information is finally becoming more available on the Internet, it is often found only through extremely specific queries, and it's hard to know what to ask about. Sometimes the information you find appears to disagree with other sources that also seem authoritative. The casual reader or prospective buyer is most likely to stumble upon the information they need by accident, if they find it at all. This guide will introduce many aspects of the subject, and if specific points are of particular interest or concern, you will have a focus to seek further information.

This is not a specific guide for particular brands or models, which are introduced and disappear at a dizzying rate anyway, but rather an assistant to help you understand the way that a pellet stove will interact with your home, budget, and lifestyle. These factors determine if "pelleting" will be the best investment you've ever made, or an exercise in frustration. I am a huge fan of using pellet stoves for home heating, but there were certainly some "warts" on the experience, as well as some unexpected pleasures when I got my stove. Even though I had researched as much information as I could find before purchasing my stove, there were still some elements of the experience that caught me off-guard. My goal is to help you decide whether this is a viable option to pursue, and to make the experience as smooth and surprise-free as possible.

I'll present an introduction to the benefits and drawbacks of particular stove design features, along with information about many of the practical concerns and planning needs of prospective stove buyers/owners. There are discussions of various features to look for in the stoves you'll consider, which should help you determine what their effect will be. I'll present a section on the comfort of your home and how it relates to your choice of heating system. There is a section to help you determine how beneficial a pellet stove would be in terms of your home layout and size, as well as information that will help you understand how to get an appropriately-sized stove for your needs. There's discussion about the expense of pellet stoves in relation to other heat sources. Pellet storage options, operating procedures, safety, and maintenance are also discussed. All of these factors will be an important part of your daily life during heating season.

In addition, there's a comparison of the experience of pellet-fueled heating with a number of other alternative and conventional home heating sources, and an extensive emphasis on those of you considering moving from woodstoves to pellet heating. There is a discussion of the controls found on modern pellet stoves, leading to how they affect stove operation, comfort, and economy.

In short, these are the answers to your questions that are NOT in the glossy sales brochures the salesperson didn't think to tell you and that you didn't even know that you should be asking and you'd wished you'd known! I want to prepare you for the experience that you can expect if you decide to get one of these great stoves.

As you read this, please keep in mind that I am not employed in any way by the pellet stove industry. I have a career spanning four decades in computer software design and development, and, in my view, the same principles used in my daily profession apply to owning a pellet stove and making it a part of your daily life. Understanding of the problem, as well as appreciating how well a solution fits the problem, efficiency, simplicity, and proper design, is important in setting up either computer software or a home heating system, and in either case, poor—or simply uninformed—decisions can drastically affect your satisfaction with the results.

Writing this guide has been inspired chiefly by the pleasure my family has gotten from owning our pellet stove, as well as discussions with people indicating there is widespread misconception about pellet stoves and how they function. If you are reading this, you are likely better informed than other folk, but the level of knowledge in the general population reminds me of when cell phones (and the Internet) were first introduced. Many folks back then didn't think that there was a need or desire for a phone you carried with you—there was always a pay phone a few blocks over!—and who would want to read "e-mail"—whatever that is—on a computer screen, anyway? I'll bet by now, 2012, that you probably know at least one person that owns a cell phone, or even has an Internet connection and computer in their home!

Unfortunately, there's quite a bit of misinformation floating around. Pellet stove websites abound with wonderfully authoritative junk, "informing" the consumer that some model of their stove will heat a 1,600 square foot house. Their bigger model? 1,900 square feet. Um, what about WHERE that house is located? Maybe the stove will heat a 1,600 ft. house in Savannah, but maybe NOT in Saskatchewan. What about how well the house is insulated? Ice fishing houses are not as easy to heat as LEED-certified buildings. Three-story buildings heat differently than one-story, even with the same footage. In many cases, you need to step beyond the claims, and evaluate for yourself. "One-size-fits-all" is not a guarantee of happiness when it comes to home heating.

Currently, quite a few folks still seem to think that pellet stoves are entirely owned by hippies living in yurts over by Woodstock somewhere, although every year, I see a few more homes on my street with suspicious-looking pallets in their driveways. I don't believe that we're ever likely to see the day when pellet stoves are as pervasive as cell phones or the Internet—for a variety of reasons—but the technology of pellet stoves is maturing rapidly, and there are compelling reasons why they will be a major driving force in the home heating market in the years to come.

If you are 'on the fence' about purchasing a pellet stove, and this guide convinces you that you absolutely MUST have one RIGHT NOW, I've done my job. I think pellet stoves are an excellent investment for improving the comfort of our homes, helping our budgets, and providing local jobs in the community, as well as strengthening the U.S. energy economy. It's hard to imagine a purchase my family and I have been happier with. However, I appreciate that they're not perfectly suited for everybody, and in this guide I've tried to present a realistic picture of stove ownership—speed bumps and all.

If this guide convinces you that a pellet stove is really NOT right for you and your family, then that's a great outcome as well. If a pellet stove is not right for your living space, your lifestyle or your physical capacity, then it's better you understand that up front, rather than waste the time, money, and effort needed to try it out. The best 'salesmen' for these stoves are the many happy and enthusiastic customers that own them, but if you're not going to be pleased with the changes and challenges this technology brings to your home, it's better to know sooner rather than later.

There's some terminology that I'll be using in this guide, and you can bet that any stove dealer or a sales brochure will incorporate a lot of the same terms too. In case you don't know, a BTU ("British Thermal Unit") is a unit of heat, and not a very big one. To put it into perspective, in order to heat a can of soup on your stove, you need about a hundred of them. To heat your home for a week, your stove (or oil furnace) might have to cough up a million or more. It's the English system equivalent of the Joule used in the metric system, even though most of us are more familiar with the "calorie". I've never seen computations of heating load on homes or buildings in terms of calories, and virtually everything you see gives the heat output of furnaces, stoves, and even cooking stove burners in terms of BTUs. In fact, what these figures actually mean is "BTUs per hour". It tells you how much heat a device can give off in a certain amount of time. A rating of "BTUs" by itself would be meaningless—a candle burning (if we had one that didn't burn down) would eventually give off a million BTUs—over the course of a year or maybe six. Some European-designed stoves are rated in terms of kilowatt-hours of heat production; with apologies to European readers, I'm leaving you to waddle through the BTUs. Figuring the equivalence should be relatively straightforward.

Your home loses heat in terms of BTUs per hour as well, determined mostly by the size of your house, the weather, the number of people per day that open and close doors, and how well it's insulated, sealed, and draft-proofed. We're trying to find the combination of heating appliances that will balance that heat requirement and provide at least enough heat to replace what the house loses when it's cold outside, leaving the inside at a pleasant temperature. Let's see how a pellet stove fits into this scenario.

Let's start with the basic definition of what a pellet stove is, and how it works. These topics will be fleshed out later, in perhaps more detail than you care to read about! For now, in its basic form, a freestanding pellet stove is an appliance that burns compressed wood (or other dried biomass) pellets, and is fed automatically by a motorized auger from a built-in pellet reservoir or hopper. A very small quantity of pellets is burning at any time, about a handful or so, in a small container called a "burn pot". For the purpose of this guide, I'll restrict this definition a bit further to "stoves that have some form of integrated temperature control mechanism, and are of suitable size for use in a residential setting". Virtually anything you can buy today as a consumer falls into this category. I'm specifically NOT going to write about early models of pellet stove, which were lacking one or more modern features that are necessary for getting the full benefit of this type of sophisticated heating system.

Another subject that will only be touched lightly is the variety of wood pellet furnaces and boilers that are coming to market as complete central-heating replacements, although the discussions of conventional central heating in here may prove instructive for those choosing that route. Those types of system comprise a large enough subject to richly deserve a dedicated work of their own.

Pellet stove design has advanced significantly since the first biomass-fired models became available some 30 years ago, mostly in the area of well-designed on-board computer controls and better understanding of a consumer's lifestyle and preferences. Early bio-fuel stoves were very "hands on", requiring manual ignition and regular tending to keep them running. They were nearly a full-time job for a dedicated tinkerer; hardly a consumer product at all.

In the last 10 or 15 years, the safety and ease of use of these stoves has improved greatly, to where they are useable by a far greater spectrum of owners. You find automatic igniters on almost all models, allowing the stoves far greater convenience, as well as utility outside the main heating season. Stove efficiency has also increased significantly. In agricultural areas in particular, similar stoves capable of burning diverse biomass products are becoming popular; the fuels include dried corn kernels, shells from peanuts and other nuts, olive or cherry pits, and various grass and fiber products. In fact, a number of the first biomass stoves did not use wood pellets at all; the "original" pellets were dried seed corn kernels. Many of the topics in this guide are applicable directly to multi-fuel stoves, but the primary focus here is wood pellets. only Ꝉ

While some folks consider a pellet stove to be interchangeable with wood stoves, as they look similar on the outside and both burn wood in some form, the inside mechanisms are very different. A simple wood stove can be little more than a cast iron box, with an opening for airflow and feeding wood, and an exhaust. More modern wood stoves are equipped with elaborate heat exchangers, catalytic combustors, and fans to help distribute hot air and increase efficiency, but are still relatively simple. In contrast, a pellet stove has a storage area, feed mechanism to fetch the pellets, and a "burn pot" where the pellets are lit and burned. There are two separate air systems with blowers on a pellet stove. One supplies combustion air directly to the burning pellets and forces the exhaust products out; the other is responsible for passing room air over the heat exchangers, thus distributing the heat to your home. The two air systems are completely sealed off from each other, to ensure that combustion gases don't enter the home.

In order to increase safety and to help with burn efficiency, pellet stoves are equipped with sensors connected to the control computer that can detect the exhaust temperature; as well as vacuum sensors that ensure that there are no defective gaskets or the stove doesn't run with a door open, and micro-switches to tell if a hopper isn't properly closed. All sensors connect to the main control computer and monitor each aspect of the stove's operation. As an example, when the stove igniter is turned on, a timer starts in the computer. If the exhaust temperature sensor fails to reach a preset temperature within a certain number of minutes, the computer decides there is a problem and will call for the stove to shut down. A number of conditions could cause this; if the burn pot fouls with ash deposits, perhaps not enough combustion air is getting in; or it could be that the igniter is failing. The exhaust sensors also provide feedback to the computer as to whether to boost or lessen the auger feed rate to maintain a steady heat output.

While the pellet stove is indeed more complex than a wood stove, the interaction of the computer with the various sensors and control mechanisms makes it extremely safe and most stoves offer several different modes of operation so that you can choose one that suits your preferences.

Finally, if you're not familiar with pellets themselves, here is a quick definition: they are sawdust or ground-up wood compressed and extruded under high pressure and heat until the wood's own internal 'lignin' glue holds them together. The manufacturing and drying process leaves the pellets with extremely low moisture content, usually 2 to 4 percent. A wood pellet contains nothing but wood; even much of the bark is removed before creating pellets, since bark does not burn as well as heartwood and produces more ash and undesirable by-products. They can be made of softwoods such as pine, hemlock, or fir, or hardwoods like oak or maple, or contain a mixture of both. Pellets are about the same appearance and size as rabbit food pellets, and because of their small and fairly uniform size, they can be moved, pumped, and poured almost like a liquid, but they can also be stacked conveniently in bags without concern for leakage as with propane or oil. There's a lot to learn about all of these subjects, so let's get started!

WHY WOULD I WANT ONE OF THESE CONTRAPTIONS?

Successful and happy ownership of a pellet stove requires a certain amount of plotting and planning to ensure that the new owners and their home are a good match with a chosen stove. There are physical demands on the owners, maintenance schedules, and some requirements on the physical layout of your home and yard, as well as some institutional challenges. In almost all cases, these challenges can be overcome, but it is important to first understand more about the stoves themselves and why we even want to bother first.

Now, why are we going to all this effort to find out about pellet stoves? Why are we even considering getting one? It's a big expense, we already have a furnace and maybe even a wood stove... why are we thinking about doing this? For years, I heard from people – "my cousin/aunt/buddy in Michigan loves his pellet stove..." but nobody had a lot of firsthand knowledge, or could express why they liked them very well. With apologies, I'm going to let my inner-computer-geek shine through for just a moment, and point out the various parts of the *"value proposition"* for pellet stoves. For you non-techno-geeks, that's an incredibly obscure way of saying "What's so great about these things?" I promise I'll try to write the rest of the book in English.

I'll cover most of these subjects in quite a bit of detail, but I'll summarize the major reasons here and get them off my chest. One, you can save boatloads of money on heating your home during winter, with complete payback on the cost of a stove and installation in just two or three years in many cases; after that it's just money in the bank. Two, it's an environmentally responsible way of heating, reducing fossil fuel usage and carbon emissions. Three, it helps our country and local area's economy create jobs and reduces our trade deficits to oil-producing countries. Still, my personal favorite is number four: it makes your house a lot more comfortable to live in than just about any other type of heating system that has ever been developed. Let's check out these outlandish claims.

BUDGET, ROUND ONE

A pellet stove in your home is almost certainly going to save you a brick of money compared with whatever heats your home now. OK, maybe. It actually depends a good deal on where you live. I live in New England, where conventional heat in the form of propane, natural gas, and home heating oil is astronomically expensive. Oil and propane prices hovered slightly above or below $3.50 per gallon in January of 2012, and were at a similar level for the last several years. Reports from some other areas in the Midwest and South indicate that recent oil and propane prices during this same period were at around $2.00 a gallon. Get ME some of that!!! Another factor is your local climate. I've corresponded with folks in the Mid-Atlantic and Mid-Pacific states who are finding pellet heat economically attractive, but payback time in a warmer climate with lower heating requirements is obviously going to be a slower process.

Anyway, I'm going to let you know how to calculate the relative prices for conventional heating vs. pellet heating. If you're in the lucky "under $2 for heating oil" crowd, justifying pellet heat solely on economic grounds is likely to turn out somewhat iffy. Still, there are other reasons to find pellet heat attractive, but this section is strictly devoted to your hard-earned bucks, and if this is going to be a first-round winner on the budget alone.

1 TIME SAV'g

Right off the bat, one thing you may qualify for are tax credits, state and/or federal. As these benefits have varied over the years and by location, consultation with a tax adviser is probably a good idea; in particular, purchasing one either immediately before, or waiting until after New Year's may net you some extra tax benefits, as the rules tend to change at year's end. This will not generate ongoing savings, but may take a bit of the sting of purchasing and installing your stove. However, let's move on to savings that will keep on coming year after year.

In most of the Northeast and many other parts of the northern US, heating with wood (either pellets or firewood) is likely to save you a real stack of Benjamins, every year, compared with conventional heat. Some of the reasons for this are pretty simple; for instance, you can look up on the net a variety of fuel-cost calculators to get an idea how much raw BTUs cost for a wide variety of fuel types. When you enter the current cost for a gallon of heating oil, a cord of wood, and a ton of pellets, the website computes the relative cost, usually in terms of "per million BTUs". If you tell your friends that you had a $600 heating bill last January that actually means that you needed to buy a certain number of BTUs to keep your home comfortable.

All heating fuels produce a fairly characteristic number of BTUs when burned, and the fuel calculators try to make sense out of the different units. There are gallons of fuel oil, versus cords of wood, therms or gallons of propane or natural gas, tons of pellets, and/or kWh of electric heat, all reduced to how many dollars a million BTUs of heat cost while burning a particular fuel. This is turn is affected by how efficient your heating system is, since a super-efficient heating system will keep more of the BTUs you bought inside your living area, instead of sending it up the chimney. In fact, Google several of the heating calculators up and compare what you get, because they all use different starting assumptions for the BTU values of various fuels and appliance efficiency, and a surprising number I tested were just plain broken. One website I found computed that you could get the heat equivalent of an entire cord of firewood (roughly 2 tons) by purchasing 17 cents worth of heating oil—about a teacup's worth. It would be very cool, if it were only true. More like di-lithium crystals, ala Star Trek.

So, in short, find a couple of fuel cost calculators; the ones at hearth.com/econtent/index.php/articles/fuel_cost_comparison_calc ulator/ and pelletheat.org/pellets/compare-fuel-costs/ seem to work pretty well, but would recommend experimenting with others you find as well. Ensure that the efficiencies for each type of appliance are realistic; some calculators I see start with extremely unrealistic (either low or high) efficiency values if they are trying to make their product seem a bit more competitive. As there don't seem to be any modern heat appliances using any type of fuel that are too far outside the range of 75-90% efficiency, if a site owner aims to convince you that their gadget runs at 96% efficiency, and their competitor's gadget runs at 47% efficiency, take that with a healthy dose of skepticism. Anyway, averaging the results from a couple of BTU calculators should give you a ballpark figure of the relative fuel cost. Ignore the folks with the 17 cents equals a cord of wood figure if you run across them in your search, and drop them an email suggesting they take remedial kindergarten math before they attempt another website.

Whatever its accuracy, any basic calculator will tell you that wood pellet heat gives you raw BTUs as cheap or cheaper than just about any heat source except coal; firewood is usually close, just a bit above or below. Swell, except that it's not the complete story by any means. Bookmark a calculator you like for later on.

Oddly, most of the reasons wood pellet heat is such a great way to save money are NOT nearly as simple as comparing BTU values for different fuels. If you look back at your calculator values, I'll let you know right now that the only value on the calculator that gives a realistic true cost comparison to pellet heat is the value for electric baseboard heat. OK, maybe coal as well. Hmmmm, I just realized that I'll need to say quite a bit more about how heating systems work before the above actually makes sense.

Pellet stoves require electrical power at all times to run, and this should be considered in the budgeting process. I measured my setup with an electrical usage meter, and found that the ignition sequence draws about 350 Watt for a few minutes, but that is typically only a few times each week. During normal operation, it draws between 100 and 150 Watt, depending on how much heat is required. Using the meter's built-in calculator, this turns out to be about 15 to 18 dollars a month in electric usage, even considering New England's astonishingly high electric rates. In other areas, you'll probably see about a 10 to 12 dollar increase on your monthly bill during the heating season. Considering the rest of the budget picture, you'll still come out far ahead.

Operational characteristics of these stoves, your daily habits, and the stove's physical placement in your home can be huge factors in driving the true cost of heating to a much lower level than you would expect. Evaluating the cost savings of these stoves is complicated by quite a number of factors, which we'll examine soon. After some more groundwork is laid, I'll illustrate how to 'fudge' the calculators to get a more realistic—and usually much more optimistic—view of how much these pellet appliances can save. In other words, pellet stove heat is likely to be even more economical than the calculators indicate. While saving money is important, we'll now see that other considerations can be equally important to your satisfaction.

COMFORT & HOW HEATING SYSTEMS WORK

To understand how pellet stoves can be so utterly swell, we need to get a better understanding of the workings of pellet systems, as well as the conventional heating systems we're currently trying to co-exist with, or replace. We also have to understand the mechanisms that control the heat sources. Not to mention that there's even a bit of plain old human psychology involved.

Let's first consider the difference between pellet stove heat and typical conventional heating systems. If you asked many folks on the street what type of heating system produces the most even, comfortable, and pleasant 'climate control' in a home, it's likely to be a no-brainer. Everyone knows that's a forced-hot-water system baseboard system running off an oil, natural gas, or propane furnace/boiler, right? At least that's the conventional wisdom in this area of the country. Most new construction here has this type of heating system installed. My own house has a propane furnace/boiler as well. It's a very popular option, and in fact, tends to be a pretty workable system. Other central heating systems—forced hot air, even electric—have their advocates as well. A majority of people think that, operating expense aside, a central heating system of some sort will leave your house about as comfortable as it could possibly be. Just goes to show you that you can fool most of the people, at least some of the time.

However, I'm letting you in on a secret—for a sense of exquisite comfort and coziness in your home that your friends will all envy; you can't do much better than wood pellet heat. I'll go into the reasons for this in excruciating detail in the following sections. Hang in there as I'm about to swerve off the main road for a bit.

Now, for some odd reason, I'd like to talk about microwave ovens. Everyone is familiar with the typical microwave oven found in most kitchens and offices. On most models, you can set a control to a variable power level, perhaps 20%, 50%, or 80% power, or the 'defrost' cycle. With the typical microwave oven design, you can actually watch how this works. When running at 50% power, most microwaves actually run at full power for 10 seconds or so, and then they shut off completely—the interior light is on and the carousel rotates, but the microwave generator itself is off—for the next 10 seconds or so, and then the oven resumes heating for the next 10 seconds, and so on. On most models you can even watch this: place a small bowl of water in the oven, set it for a few minutes at 50% power level, and once the water boils, you'll see it boil furiously for a few seconds, then stop completely, then boil furiously, then stop, over and over. You can even hear the on-off cycles. The fan picks up speed when the power is not going to the microwave generator. The fan goes MMMM-mmmm-MMMM-mmmm-MMMM-mmmm, right? 100% plus 0% averages out to 50%. Yeah, it's not very satisfactory in cooking your food, and it's not a completely satisfactory way to heat your home, either.

Here's a quick tip completely unrelated to pellet stoves; unlike the rest of the microwave oven manufacturers, the nice folk at Panasonic make microwave oven models that actually change the intensity of microwaves that hit your food. In other words, the "60% power" setting actually delivers 60% power, rather than "on high for 10 seconds, off for 5". It seems to be unique in the market; I've owned one for five or six years now, and it and beats the stuffing out of any of the dozen other microwaves I've owned or used, as it delivers the proper amount of heat required for slower cooking and is excellent at defrosting food without roasting it.

Most microwave ovens are of the "dumb" kind, however, and I'll refer to that sort going forward. So, what makes a heating system so similar to a "dumb" microwave oven?

The typical on-off-on-off microwave behavior is exactly like most of the conventional heating systems installed in homes today. The working principle of such systems is that the thermostat in the home reaches a certain preset level a couple of degrees below the desired comfort level, and the heating system is turned on at full maximum power. Once the temperature in the home reaches a certain level, a couple of degrees above the desired comfort level, the heating system is turned completely off. You set the thermostat at 70 degrees, and the temperature wanders back and forth all day and all night between 68 degrees and 72 degrees. So, while your central system keeps your house within a particular "comfort range", in reality, the temperature is constantly swinging back and forth between a little bit too cold and a little bit too warm. In fact, the thermostat's temperature range between its "on" and "off" points is referred to as the "swing".

It's like that microwave: while the heat cycle is on your food may be burning, and when the microwave is off, no heat is being transferred to the food at all. Your typical furnace does the same—it is blasting heat for 15 minutes, then shuts down completely for half an hour. I think of these heating systems as being in 'microwave-mode'. They keep the house somewhere close to being at a comfortable temperature, but because they produce heat either far in excess, or not at all, the time when the house is 'just perfect' amounts to only a few minutes a day. About all we can say about this is that it's great that we aren't outside freezing in a snowdrift, but comfort takes a back seat when using these schizophrenic on-off heat systems. Surely, we can do better.

THE FAMOUS THERMOSTAT ROLLER COASTER! THRILLS AND CHILLS!

Now, pellet stoves are an example of what I call a "continuous heating appliance". This type of appliance can deliver an overall greater level of even and uniform temperature comfort in the home, while most conventional sources of 'central' heat (oil, propane, natural gas, electric) leave us pining for springtime and a vacation in the Florida Keys. Pellet stoves keep an almost perfectly stable temperature in your home because they produce exactly the amount of heat that is required at any given time and adjust automatically to provide it. If it's really cold, they toss a lot of heat; if it's only chilly, they produce just a little. This is an incredible advance in heating systems. How is this possible? It's time to realize that 'conventional' heating systems rely on technology that is rapidly approaching the one and a half century mark. Think about it. Your cell phone is 18 months old? Oooh, it's a dinosaur, hustle down to Verizon or AT&T for a trade-in on the latest Android or iPhone. Yet you're satisfied with a home heating system that was perfected when Teddy Roosevelt was President? Excuse me??

We should have a chat about our old buddy, the thermostat. It is pretty much unchanged since invented by Edison, or maybe it was Galileo, or Fred Flintstone? Actually, Wikipedia has a nice article on thermostats; and yes, they really haven't changed their basic function since they were first invented more than 130 years ago. It's a simple on/off switch, with a high and a low "swing" temperature limit. Once the low limit is reached, the heat source is turned on, and runs at maximum blast until the upper limit is reached, and then the heat source is turned off completely. There's no "dimmer switch" function possible to get the heat output that will keep your home's temperature stable. Remember us talking about microwave ovens? This is why in every type of thermostat-controlled system the temperature is never stable; it's always rising or falling. Still, there are some pellet stoves that come with thermostats only, but these are typically relegated to ultra-discount and big-box stores. Clearly, these have most of the disadvantages of the central-heat 'microwave-mode' heating systems, and then some. These are really poor candidates for a home-heat system, although they may be fine for taking the chill off the barn when you're milking the cows! This also gives you a clue as to why some pellet stoves sell for thousands of dollars less than high-end models. "Gosh, I saw a swell pellet stove at Big Box Giant for only $899!" Yup, a bargain for sure, unless you count comfort, maintainability, and availability of parts if you need them.

Am I really being fair to the thermostat? After all, you can now get cool programmable thermostats that can do full 7-day schedules with multiple changes each day. Pretty nifty, eh! So, your daytime "programmed temperature" is 68, and it automatically sets back to 65 at night. So, that means that during the day your temperature wobbles between 66 and 70, back and forth constantly, and at night the temperature bobs and weaves from 63 to 67. It saves a few bucks on heating oil, but is a giant goose egg as far as increasing comfort. Recently, an ex-Apple guy was heavily marketing an "intelligent" thermostat that incorporated a motion detector to see if you're home, so that it can automatically adjust its daily settings, and even allows you to connect to it over the internet. But what does it do with all that computer power and intelligence? Turns your furnace ON full blast, and then OFF again, so now your discomfort is intelligently planned by the Internet. Oh, joy.

Nearly every consumer conventional home heating system ends up working the same way, no matter how high-tech. If you drive somewhere in your car, would you accelerate to 60, coast until it stops, and accelerate again to 60 and coast again? After all, you'd get there in about the same time as if you just drove all the way at 30. But somehow, doesn't sound that comfortable to me.

So, here's the deal: for many of you that take the plunge, a pellet stove is not going to be just a little auxiliary source of heat, like an occasional fire in the hearth to take off the chill. "Oooh, cute, how about a nice chilled glass of Chardonnay with that?" NOT. A pellet stove is going to muscle its way into your home and heart as the primary way your house gets heat. If you get a high-quality modern brand of pellet stove, it is very likely to become your "main squeeze" as a heat source. In that case, it's worthwhile getting the best quality and features you can afford, because it's going to make you forget about your "old love"—oil/gas heating system.

Here's where a good brand of pellet stove with modern controls really shows its superiority to other heating systems. Higher quality pellet units have what is usually called a "room temperature sensor", although it could be called by other names, such as "comfort monitor" or "temperature wizard". Whatever! It is NOT a thermostat. Read the literature on the stove you're considering, and see if the stove's controls do what a temperature sensor does. Even if the sales rep tells you it's a thermostat, it might not be; some sales folk I've run into are confused on the concept too! To some of them, whatever regulates temperature in some fashion is automatically called a thermostat. One model I looked at had a temperature sensor with a built-in control computer that could be placed up to 75 feet away from the actual stove, and the unit looked exactly like a programmable thermostat, even though it was actually a very sophisticated heat-sensor unit!

So, what makes a "temperature sensor" so different from a thermostat? And how does that difference make it somehow better? Because of the computer attached to it! The computer checks the temperature from the sensor, and keeps track of the temperature trends in the home. If the temperature is dropping or rising fast, it understands that and adjust the stove output. If only a small amount of heat is needed to maintain a constant temperature, it understands that too. A proper pellet stove is pretty much infinitely variable in

(handwritten margin notes:) NOT A THERMOSTAT BUT

(handwritten margin note:) HEAT SENSOR UNIT

(handwritten note:) REGULATES pellet flow

(handwritten margin note:) DITTO

heat output, so if the temperature is dropping rapidly, the computer will signal the stove to boost its heat output dramatically and quickly by increasing the rate it trickles pellets into the burn pot and bumping up the heat distribution fan. If the room temperature is pretty steady or is starting to rise, the computer can slow the trickle to almost nothing—just a "maintenance burn", while still producing only about the same heat as a couple of candles.

In fact, your home heating system is the only heat control system you own that exhibits this wacky on/off behavior. Walking outside and a breeze comes up? Zip up your jacket a couple inches. Get too warm? Zip it down a few inches. Adjust, frequently, in small amounts. It's the key to comfort. If your jacket was controlled by a thermostat, you'd have to take it off completely until you were freezing, then put it back on zipped up to your chin until you were too hot to stand it, and then take it off again. A kitchen range has a dial to regulate the amount of heat each burner produces, so your omelet cooks at the correct rate. Your car's heater has a dial that adjusts how much heat comes out of the vents, so that you can remain comfortable on your commute to work. Everywhere you look, the key to comfort is adjustability, that is EXCEPT your home heating system, running on 1883 technology. So, whatever they call the adjustment mechanism, if the pellet stove you're considering can adjust its heat output level based on how much heat is required, it has a temperature sensor. If it adjusts to different heat output levels automatically, it is NOT controlled by a thermostat. Thermostats go ON, and they go OFF. Period. They do NOT adjust heat output, ever.

While your typical residential living-room thermostat regulating your furnace can allow 3 to 4 degree temperature swings in the room, at least one brand of pellet stove advertises that its temperature-sensor system will hold your room temperature constant to within one-half of a degree. This is why pellet systems are some of the most comfortable heating sources you can install. The temperature will just stay precisely where you set it. You feel better and cozier when the room temperature doesn't keep changing every minute! Until someone develops an adjustable-output central furnace that is coupled with a temperature sensor and a computer, pellet heat is going to provide you with a more comfortable living area.

While we're on the subject, wood stoves also have the ability to stabilize temperature to a more limited degree, and provide at least some of the temperature-steadying effect that pellet stoves have. You can throw in more wood as it gets colder, or reduce the air supply to regulate the heat if it's getting too warm. You, together with your wood stove, are doing a crude version what the temperature sensor and computer do in the pellet unit—adjusting heat output to match the temperature trends in the home. If the house is running mostly on conventional heat, a wood stove chugging along at a low level will slow the descent to the thermostat kick-on temperature. And yes, that's one of the big reasons many folks love wood heat. Conventional wood stove heat really is pretty comfortable. It helps cushion the relatively large, uncomfortable temperature oscillations inherent in every thermostat-controlled system. But a good pellet stove computer adjusts heat output minute-by-minute to stabilize your home temperature far better than a wood stove, and thermostat-controlled central heating systems are strictly third rate in any comparison in terms of comfort.

So, it turns out that pellets may be a winning solution for you, as an individual family, as you can not only save some money, but have your house a lot nicer to live in. Sweet! Still, like many choices we make, there are effects on the larger picture—our community, employment, our immediate environment, and the planet. So, is running a pellet stove going to drive a few endangered species into oblivion? Wipe out coral reefs in the Galapagos? Make the breadlines of the 1930s seem like banquets? Make Chernobyl's environmental disaster seem like a Boy Scout picnic? Fortunately, adopting a pellet heat system has many positive effects on society, in all of these areas.

ENVIRONMENTAL CONCERNS

Pellet fuel is excellent in terms of greenhouse gas efficiency if you are concerned about climate change. The carbon cycle for pellet fuel is primarily local. Trees grow in your area, and extract carbon dioxide from the air, eventually mature, are harvested and turned into pellet fuel, then burned, producing more carbon dioxide, which is then taken up by new trees. And this cycle repeats itself. The cycle is not 100% greenhouse gas efficient, because there are harvesting, manufacturing, and transportation costs to consider, typically using a certain quantity of fossil fuels. Some folks have the conception that as soon as you burn firewood or pellets, the carbon dioxide released is immediately sucked up by the dandelions in the yard, and that there is no effect on the atmosphere, but unfortunately that's not really accurate. There is an ongoing debate as to whether the carbon released by pellet stoves is reclaimed by vegetation growth as quickly as once thought, some studies indicating the carbon-payback time may be 10 to 30 years before the pellets you burn today become part of new plant, tree, and algae growth. Other studies suggest that burning wood in a high-efficiency stove may actually contribute LESS to greenhouse gases than allowing the wood to decay naturally, as that produces a mix of both carbon dioxide and some methane, and methane is a much more powerful contributor to warming than carbon dioxide. While there's obviously some uncertainty about pellet's carbon cycle, contrast that with how long it's going to be before the carbon dioxide from your oil furnace exhaust is going to be brand new oil. What, maybe 25 million years? 50 million?

There is also some question about sustainability of our forests. Are pellet stoves going to denude all of the forests of New England and the Far West? Well, no. Fortunately, the sustainable output of wood, and wood waste, from our forests far exceeds the current and projected demand. Just the amount of deadfall from a single hurricane dwarfs the amount of wood consumed by the pellet industry. And in Europe, creative thinking is bringing about synergistic processes where tree farms can be irrigated with partially purified wastewater, yielding much lower costs for community wastewater processing and yielding wood pellets that the community can sell for a profit! Finally, the electronic revolution has meant that far less paper is being produced. People are reading newspapers online and exchanging email rather than paper mail. The magnitude of the drop in paper production alone is greater than the current amount demanded for pellet heating.

So, even considering that it's not ecologically perfect, pellet fuel is much more environmentally friendly than almost any other fuel, especially fossil derived fuels such as oil, propane, and natural gas, or electricity derived from sources such as coal or nuclear power. Pellet and other bio-fuels are renewable on a human time scale, unlike oil, gas, and coal, which are being consumed far more quickly than they are forming. Wind and solar power are important components of our energy economy, too; however, while being 'green', they are not always available when you really want them. Widespread use of pellet and bio-fuels in homes and in industrial situations will be an increasingly important part of reducing the rise of greenhouse gas emissions in the future, as well as controlling our import of foreign oil and stabilizing our local economies. Recent studies have shown that for every dollar spent on oil heat, that nearly 90 cents leaves the local economy. With pellets, nearly 90 cents STAYS in the local economy. That's the difference between billions of dollars going overseas to countries that hate us, or billions of dollars going to your neighbors and friends. There's something to like for just about everybody here in pellet-land, unless you happen to be an oil tycoon.

Conservation of energy is another important factor to consider in a pellet stove installation. Just because it's pretty cheap heat doesn't mean that you should ignore energy-saving measures. Caulking cracks, installing energy efficient windows and beefing up insulation will also help reduce the amount of heat your home needs. You can get a home energy audit performed by a local company, or sometimes your local electric or gas utility will do it free of charge; this can point out areas where you can improve your heating efficiency. Cheap solutions, such as a few tubes of caulking and "draft snakes" for your doors, will bring immediate results as far as comfort and saving heat without busting the piggy bank.

Also, don't consider the audit recommendations an "all-or-nothing" proposition. One of the best ways to improve energy efficiency in many homes is upgrading your windows. Instead of just gasping and saying "Forget it! No way!" when they quote you a price in excess of 10 thousand dollars to makeover your whole house, develop a five-year plan. Replace only a couple of the worst windows this year, then use the money you save with your pellet stove to buy a couple more next year, and so on. In a matter of perhaps five years, the house will be completely done, and you won't have had the sticker-shock of doing it all at once. Not to mention that, with each passing year of the plan, the house will get more comfortable AND cheaper to run.

One eco-question most pellet stove owners have sooner or later is: What do we do with all those plastic pellet bags? Aren't they an environmental nightmare? Well, it's not quite that bad. Firstly, many of you can recycle them. Our local pellet company points out that their bags are manufactured from the same plastic as grocery bags, and most grocery stores have recycling bins for any bags made of that plastic these days. And if you consider the amount of oil that you DON'T burn when you burn a ton of pellets instead (hint: at least 150+ gallons), a gallon or so of oil to make the bags that the pellets came in seems to be relatively small potatoes. We also use the bags occasionally as trash bags, or whenever we need a really tough piece of plastic, and the large bags that cover each ton of pellets can be used to shelter my snowblower, generator, or lawnmower.

LOCAL ECONOMY AND JOBS

This one's a no-brainer. Just about all of the ongoing operating cost of a wood pellet or biomass stove goes straight into your local economy. A study I recently came across indicated that fossil fuel-based energy consumption sends more than 90% of the revenue OUT of the local area, so your local economy benefits very little. Pellets are largely produced close to your home, because it's not usually very economical to ship them more than a couple hundred miles. Nobody's importing 40-pound bags of pellets from Saudi Arabia, China, or Malaysia and driving up our trade deficits. Agricultural producers near you may be able to sell biomass fuels such as nutshells or cherry pits that were previously considered waste products and a liability. Many sawmills find that being able to sell their waste wood instead of paying to dispose of it is the difference between red and black on the balance sheet. The need for forestry workers and production crews for pellet plants will also increase. Not to mention that if you, the stove owner, have a bit more folding green in your pocket because it's cheaper to heat with pellets, that's not a bad thing for the local economy either.

While we're on the subject, if you're going for a pellet-fueled future, do yourself and your country's economy a favor and consider getting a unit made in your own country (American-made for me), as long as a knowledgeable local dealer stands behind the brand and offers spare parts and service. Some units made in Canada, Scandinavia, Germany, France, China, and elsewhere have excellent reputations, parts availability and dealer networks as well. Regardless of origin, I think it's essential to get a brand that has a large following, good reputation, and a big presence in the market. Good units are extremely reliable, but if you need parts or warranty service, you'll be ahead of the game when the new parts don't have to come by slow freight from Shanghai or Moscow, and the distributor's head office isn't in the Deep South (of Brazil) somewhere. Somehow, that nice woman on the customer service line in Atlanta (or Calcutta) won't have the same sense of urgency as you do in Vermont with the wind chill at -15 F. and dropping. Being without your pellet stove for 12 weeks in winter can easily make that money you saved buying it at George's Fly-by-Night Bargain Store evaporate without a trace.

In any case, it's worthwhile doing some research to see how the brand and model of stove you are considering holds up over time. Online forums are a great source of community opinion on these matters, as many contributors will have experience with the stove model you're thinking about purchasing. While you're there, ask about the dealers in your area and find out if people have been happy with them. Some dealers have earned a reputation for being, shall we say, a trifle less than helpful with warranty servicing, and some refuse to work on stoves not purchased from them, even when they carry the same brand. Look in the yellow pages, and you'll see that the number of pellet stove dealers that you'll need to ring up for service someday is pretty small compared to the number of places that can service your gas furnace. If there are only one or two pellet dealers in your area and you don't get a good vibe from them, it may not be your time to get a pellet stove just yet. Businesses come and go for reasons as random and simple as a death in the family, so it's a good idea to see if you'll be left high-and-dry if there are no other dealers that can handle repairs and pellet supply in your area.

WILL IT WORK FOR ME?

PELLET STORAGE — *IMPORTANT CONSIDERA'N*

One big thing that's a practical concern for prospective pellet stove owners is the storage of pellets themselves. It can be a real deal-breaker for in-city or apartment dwellers—small yards, no garage, no place to put the pellets? Oil's easy, as the tank is in the basement! Natural gas? A one-inch pipe in from the street. Wood pellets—now what? It's one of the most important, and most often ignored, considerations when contemplating owning a pellet stove, so let's mull that over now.

When purchasing pellets, the most common arrangement is that the pellets will arrive on a truck, and you will need to have a spot to place between four and six tons of pellets, as this is a fairly typical winter's supply around here. Each ton of pellets occupies a floor space approximately 4' x 4', and is 4 feet high. Some places sell larger 1.5 ton pallets, which are just a foot or two taller and may be of interest if you have a very limited stacking area. The pellets are usually unloaded from the truck using a portable forklift, which requires a space at least 8-10 feet wide in order to maneuver. The space you choose to store your pellets should be out of the way of traffic and cars, where you want to park or access your garage, out of the way of snow blowers and lawn mowers. It should also be away from the street and near the house in order to discourage people from casually snatching a sack or two of your pellets or vandalizing them. If possible, they should be in a back or side yard, somewhat out of view.

4 to 6 TONS = New England winter

1 Ton = 4'x4' floor space 4' High
there are 1.5 ton pallets

33

PELLET STACKING ERRORS 101

Your storage should be convenient to the door you'll use to bring the pellets to the stove. The forklift will probably NOT be able to deliver your pellets inside a garage or shed (but check!), although if need be, the pallets can be re-stacked inside a garage or porch manually, but this requires a fair amount of heavy lifting. Friends and beer could help out here. Some pellet suppliers offer 'pallet jack' service for a small fee, so that they can move the pellets inside your garage if you have room there. Having room in the garage or basement for at least a portion of your pellets is really nice, because the pellets will stay dry unless you have a major flood, and you don't have to run outside for stove food on a morning, like today, when it's 30 degrees and freezing rain is dumping outside.

Once the forklift delivers the pellets, they are darn near impossible to move in bulk, and typically will be there until spring or until they're burned up. Placing them on a lawn will leave you with a dead spot of grass unless they get delivered after growing season. In addition, the pellets should be out of the weather if practical; in any case, never placed directly under a roof overhang where rainwater or snow/ice sliding off the roof will soak them or puncture the bags. Pellets are generally delivered in 40-pound bags, 50 per one-ton forklift pallet. The bags are plastic, but are not entirely weatherproof. Small leaks in the bags can, and do, occur, and in fact the bags have small deliberate holes to keep the bags from popping when stacked. In addition, each pallet is usually covered with a large plastic cover that fits over the whole ton (useful for covering motorcycles, generators, woodpiles, etc. after the ton is consumed).

Although it's really hard to move a whole pallet-load without heavy equipment, some folks do opt to manually re-stack the bags in a garage, basement, or enclosed porch. They report that the bags can be stacked to 8 feet or higher without damaging the bottom layers of pellets, cutting in half the floor space needed for each ton. If you decide to do this, please ensure that, if you stack more than 4 or 5 feet high, the bags are stacked neatly in a crisscross interlocking pattern and secured so that they are not prone to tipping over. Having a ton of pellets fall on you (or your car or snowmobile or bicycle or cat) will certainly screw up your day. Remember that pellets in bulk are really heavy! A single pallet of them weighs more than some small cars. Evaluate carefully how much you can safely store if you want to move some to a covered porch or deck, as there have been at least a few reports of porches or floors sagging or collapsing when an owner moved all five tons "out of the weather".

DON'T EXCEED LOAD CAPACITY OF YOUR FLOOR OR PORCH!

I strongly recommend in most areas that you place an additional plastic tarp weighted or tied down over your outdoor pellets because the pellet bags have deliberate ventilation holes and often pinholes or small tears from handling, and will leak and absorb moisture, which can cause the pellets to deteriorate. Pellets are just like little sponges and, when exposed to water, quickly sop it up, swell to more than double the original size, turn into wet sawdust and are no longer usable! But gee, come to think about it, pellets really are not like little sponges after all, because once pellets absorb water, they never dry out and go back to shape like a sponge would. For this reason, bags of pellets should always be left on their shipping pallet until they are moved inside, into a staging area (e.g. covered porch), or to the stove. One tip – if you find that a bag has a soggy blob of sawdust inside as well as viable pellets, allow the bag to freeze solid outside. Afterwards, you can discard the frozen sawdust lump and use the pellets in the bag that are still good.

Pellets remaining outside should remain under their plastic covering (and maybe an additional tarp) because sunlight can deteriorate the individual plastic bags, allowing them to weaken and split. Often, the outer bags covering the whole ton have ultra-violet blockers, which help protect the individual bags, but just about any plastic will deteriorate, get brittle, and shred after a couple of years in the sun. It's a good idea if you have pellets left over from a previous year that you rotate your stock and use them up first this year. Even if stored inside, your pellets should remain elevated off the floor to protect the bottom layer of bags from moisture. Finally, even if you store outside, having a 'staging area' in the basement, garage, or on a sheltered porch where you can keep a half-dozen bags of pellets to access easily on really cold, stormy days or late at night is a lifesaver!

Setting bags of pellets directly on the ground, pavement, or even concrete floors invites rainwater, ground moisture, or snowmelt to ruin your pellets by sucking up water through the tiny holes in the plastic bags. Because of this, if you must re-stack pellets to get them into an outdoor shed or the back yard, always stack them on extra pallets, bricks or boards to keep them a few inches off the ground.

You should ideally purchase only what you need for a single winter season or a slight bit more at a time, which will typically be 4 to 6 tons of pellets for most of us. Any leftovers will keep just fine until next winter, but with the recent crazy weather, hurricanes and flash floods near our area, I'd rather chance losing a half-ton of leftover pellets than the 12 tons that I got a super deal on last year!

Back to our city and apartment dwellers, though—talk to your local pellet suppliers if you think that pellet storage will be a problem and you otherwise want to get onto the pellet brigade. They may have solutions such as bulk-storage systems (pour into a storage bin in the basement, never have to go out in the cold for your fuel? Sign me up!). I've run across dealers on the web advertising that they would store the pellets you buy from them in their warehouse for a modest fee; you can pick them up in your Mini-Cooper, five bags at a time, when you need them. You can typically buy single 40-pound bags from dealers, but they usually cost $.50 to a dollar more per bag that way. If you only have storage space for a dozen bags at a time, it can be workable. In any case, describe your situation and brainstorm potential solutions with your dealer and friends, or check out the internet forums.

Various bulk storage systems are available, although most are oriented toward automatic feeding of whole-house pellet boiler systems. There are also soft-side bins, similar to large reinforced bags suspended from frames, which are suitable for indoor storage, as well as weatherproof rigid plastic outdoor bins. Some systems allow you to store a few tons of pellets, where you can just go to the bin and fill up a bucket of pellets from a spigot on the bottom. This is a great way to fly if you don't have the physical strength and stamina to haul in the standard 40-pound bags of pellets, as you can fill a small bucket with the quantity you can safely carry. That's also a nice option if you can't recycle your plastic pellet bags locally, since there's only so many trash bags most folks need. Ask local pellet suppliers if they can deliver in bulk and make sure that you understand how their unloading process works. Some trucks have a rigid auger system, and must be able to drive up to within 10 or 12 feet of your storage bin and have a direct shot in. However, an increasing number of dealers have pneumatic hose or vacuum pumping systems that will deliver 30 to 50 feet away. They can even pump the pellets around corners or down stairs, offering far greater flexibility in your storage bin placement. Bulk delivery may also get you a discount of 25 to 50 dollars per ton on the pellets themselves.

If you have a pickup or small truck, you can avoid delivery charges altogether by buying a ton at a time and carting it home yourself.

For whatever delivery you choose, bags or bulk, there's usually a delivery charge ranging from $25 to $100 or more to bring their truck and forklift to your home, and often it's about the same charge whether you buy one ton or five; so, when you buy several tons, the delivery charge is split and each ton effectively costs less. Also, distance is a factor in delivery; many dealers charge by the distance from their plant to your house, so buying higher cost-per-ton pellets from a local dealer may be ultimately cheaper than buying at a lower per-ton price from a distant dealer, once the delivery charges are added. There are several web-based pellet-supply companies too, which are a potential option for folks in areas with unreliable local supplies of pellets. They seem to charge flat shipping fees depending on your zip code no matter how many tons you order, as well as discounts for larger purchases, so buying your entire year's supply may turn out to be a good buy for some of you.

THUNDER AND LIGHTNING

Although not quite as noisy, pellet stoves do produce sound. And light. Most owners report that the sound that their stove makes fades into the background in a day or two. There are sounds typical of most stoves—the air distribution and combustion fans, pellets falling into the auger and burn pot, as well as the auger feeding the pellets, and each model of stove has its own "sound signature". On some models, the fans may be quieter but the feed auger produces a whine, others just the opposite. And people are different, too. A fan running may be soothing white noise to one person, yet very annoying to another. The fans may vary in speed depending on the heat load; again some folks couldn't care less, others prefer a more constant sound level.

I suggest grabbing a beach chair, and going to the dealer. Have them start a stove, so you can hear what the starting sequence sounds like, then sit down next to it for a half hour or so, and check out the sound levels. At the end of that time, you should have a better idea how well you'll adjust. Personally, I chose one of the quieter models on the market, and its sound is somewhat audible, or at least detectable, throughout much of the house when the TV and kids' music are off. It's somewhat louder than my refrigerator, and way quieter than the dishwasher! I can hear pellets dropping, the auger turning, and the blowers running. On the other hand, it's much quieter than my furnace, which has its own characteristic ignition sequence and operating sounds—exhaust fan on high, relays snapping closed, pumps circulating water to the baseboards, and the WHOOOOMP when the gas flame ignites. Relatively speaking, the pellet stove is a lullaby, but you may be more, or less, sensitive than I am.

Those familiar with wood stoves are accustomed to light, or usually lack thereof. Even wood stoves with glass fronts tend to smoke up rapidly, and you can hardly see the flames most of the time unless you clean the glass daily. Pellet stoves produce very little smoke, and the flame tends to be very visible. If I had to, I could read by the light mine gives off; I estimate it is about the equivalent of a 25 Watt light bulb. When we come home after dark, our kitchen is lit by the warm glow from the stove and looks very welcoming, which something I never experienced with the old wood stove.

The reason the sound and light are particularly relevant is that some of you are probably thinking of installing a stove in your bedroom. I'm going to try to discourage you; while it sounds nice and cozy on a cold winter night, the sound and flickering light in the room could make sleep difficult. I've slept with a fireplace or a wood stove in the room at various places we've stayed, but after an hour, the fire dies down and all is quiet and dark and perfect for sleeping. A pellet stove would annoy me all night. I have to think you'll be much happier installing the stove elsewhere in the house unless you have a very specific requirement to have the stove in the room at night. Even if you are not thinking of a bedroom installation, you'll have to decide on an appropriate spot for the stove and consider whether the sound and light levels in that spot could be distracting or disruptive. For instance, putting the stove in the same room as your home theater system might be a distraction when you want to watch a movie in the evening.

SIZING YOUR PELLET STOVE

So, if you're thinking about a pellet stove, one of the most important questions relates to its size. It's fairly easy to answer this with choosing a car: how many kids do you need to carry? How much luggage? With a pellet stove, it's not obvious; BTUs are not as easy to account for as number of car seats and cubic feet of trunk space. So, the question actually boils down to how big is big enough, and when is a BTU not a BTU? An easy answer to the size question is to get one the same BTU capacity as your furnace that heats your house now, right? Well, I suppose that could work, but it's really the wrong answer—and substantial overkill—for a number of reasons.

Firstly, most conventional heating installations suffer from an inherent inefficiency. A significant portion (up to 10-20%) of furnace and boiler heat is simply wasted in many installations, because it goes to heating your basement and escapes through the basement walls and floors. So, if you think your living space will have a maximum heat requirement of 50,000 BTUs an hour, and you're building a home with a furnace as the sole heat source, you need to account for that "lost" heat. For your 50,000 BTU "heat need", you really require a minimum of a 60,000 BTU furnace. As I'm not a heating engineer, these numbers are only an informed estimate, but you can see the principle. Again, in this example, if you were crazy enough have your furnace and all the piping smack dab in the middle of your living room, all of that "basement waste heat" would now be usable as "living space heat", and you'd only need a 50,000 BTU furnace.

In the real world, despite having tables of roof thickness, R-values, and window efficiency, heating engineers like to throw in a good safety margin for super-cold weather, unexpectedly high air leakage in a new home, a high volume of pedestrian traffic in and out, and so on. So, if their little iPad heating-calculation app coughs out a final figure for your home's "heating need" of 52,864.9328 BTUs per hour, they're likely going to tell you that you require a 120,000 BTU per hour furnace system. It's a good call; the furnace itself will add a couple hundred bucks over an 80,000 BTU model, and take up an extra 6 inches of basement space, but you are NOT going to get cold with their furnace heating your house. No risk of having irate customers calling the heating engineer at 2 AM when it's 13 below outside because the furnace won't keep up.

Our problem with the pellet stove is a bit different, though. In all likelihood, we're going to be keeping the furnace, and the pellet stove is not going to be the ONLY source of heat we can use. If you ARE thinking of using a pellet stove as your sole source of heat with no backup, you REALLY need to do a much more thorough analysis of the size of the unit you need, and going overboard is certainly better than the alternative! Assuming that it won't be your only heat source, though, you don't really need to have a pellet stove large enough to cover your coldest-windiest day ever. Around here, there's only a half dozen days in a year when the temperature is at its lowest, and if the propane or oil comes on for a few hours, it's not a huge deal.

If you DO have access to the heating folks that designed your house, by all means ask them for your home's heat loss estimates. You may even be able to find a chart of expected heat loss: 15,000 BTU/h @ 40 F, 20,000 BTU/h at 30 F, etc. However, for many of you, the heating engineer that worked on your house when it was built retired in 1892, and died shortly after Woodrow Wilson's inauguration, and their so-called planning amounted to, "Looks big 'nuff to me, back up the wagon, Jake!" Having the computed numbers will help inform your decision, but we can figure it out pretty well even without them. However, heating systems have a way of being more complicated than you may have thought.

GETTING HEAT TO WHERE YOU WANT IT

So, let's get into a bit here on figuring out how much of the heat an appliance generates can actually get to where you really want it.

We're going to imagine a (this is dumb, really silly, don't actually try this, please) scenario to see how much heat our system can actually deliver to our living space. This can actually be quite a different number than the quoted furnace "BTU capacity". Say we have a nice forced-water heating system, with a boiler powered by either gas or oil, and rated to deliver 100,000 BTUs each and every hour. Now, we go upstairs on a really nasty, cold windy day—it's 10 below zero, wind cruising by at 35 or so. Let's do something we should NEVER do—let's toss open ALL the doors and windows! Magically, let's assume our "heat need" has suddenly risen to EXACTLY 100,000 BTUs. In theory, we're still going to be warm, because the furnace is rated as capable of supplying 100,000 BTUs, of course! Ah, but remember, about 20% of that heat was going to heat the basement and is lost before it gets upstairs, so the effective size of the boiler is really only 80,000 BTUs. Let's close one or two of those windows; it's getting frigid in here! Now, assume our "heat need" has magically dropped to EXACTLY 80,000 BTUs. We should be all set now.

Except for one thing. How is the heat actually delivered into the living area? In a forced-water system, water flows through pipes in baseboards that have fins to allow the heat to escape and heat the air in the room. Those baseboards have a maximum heat-dissipation capacity. They can only give off a certain amount of heat in an hour, per foot of baseboard. Heating engineers have figures for this so that they know how much baseboard to install. To make things simple, I'm going to pick figures out of the air for this example—let's say each foot of baseboard can release 1,000 BTUs per hour, and I will assume that the house has 50 feet of baseboard. Each hour, all of the baseboards in the entire house can only release a maximum of 50,000 BTUs. Hey, what happened to our 100,000 BTU/h boiler? Well, the boiler controls monitor the internal water temperature and won't allow the water to overheat and turn to steam, but the furnace adds more heat to the water than the baseboards upstairs can get rid of. So, the boiler shuts itself off every few minutes to let the baseboard radiators dissipate the heat, and then turn on again once the water has cooled enough to start the cycle again.

If you have this type of heating system, you may remember having to heat the house up 20 degrees or so after a couple days of power outage, coming back from vacation, or maybe a furnace malfunction, right? Even though the house is still really cold, you can hear the furnace/boiler shutting down and restarting repeatedly. You're trying to stop your teeth from chattering, and your furnace keeps shutting off? Congratulations, you've just experienced the "Maximum Heat Delivery Capacity" of your heating system. If you had the patience, you could take a stopwatch and time the boiler on/off cycles for an hour, and you might find that your furnace only runs ½ of the time, even under "maximum load". So, the true maximum BTU delivery possible with our example furnace is really only ½ what we thought it was, because it has nowhere to get rid of the actual amount of heat it could create!

While the forced-water heating system we discussed above has problems delivering all of its heat, other types of heating systems are not necessarily constrained in the same fashion. Any system that uses moving air as a heat-transfer medium is able to deliver a very significant quantity of its rated output, including both pellet stoves and forced-hot-air furnaces. Wood stoves with heat-distribution fans qualify too. Why? Because the heat-transfer medium—heated air— immediately mixes with room temperature air and dissipates. In a moving hot-air system, there is effectively an unlimited supply of cool heat-transfer medium. Any type of hot-air-distribution heating system should be able to deliver fairly close to the full, rated BTU capacity (minus losses to the basement) when driven with maximum demand. In our water-based system, the transfer medium (water) is in a closed system with a fixed amount of water, and the heat transfer capacity of the baseboards can effectively limit the amount of heat we can deliver to our living space, regardless of the boiler's nominal BTU capacity.

Back to the sizing question. The basic question is not "How big is my existing furnace?" because we've shown that, under normal conditions, your furnace probably is NOT delivering heat to your living area at even close to its "book" rate, and it never would, even if it tried! If you want to try taking the heat engineer's estimate of your heat needs as a starting point, I'd suggest a pellet stove with between one-third and one-half the rated BTU capacity of your furnace as a starting "guesstimate". This coincides pretty well with the pellet stoves on the market; typical home heating systems seem to be often rated at 80,000 to 150,000 BTUs in New England, and pellet stove ratings from the manufacturers' websites start around 25,000 BTUs/hour and go up to a maximum capacity of around 70,000. While a honkin'-big stove is comforting to have (and there's really not much downside other than space it requires and the initial cost), my personal opinion is that you can supply just about all the heat you could use to any average-sized New England home with good insulation and good air circulation with a 50,000 BTU or smaller stove. In a home that is more segmented, you may not even be able to use that much capacity. There's no reason NOT to get a stove bigger than you need if it fits your space and budget, but if you've found a great deal on a used 42,000 BTU stove, or the monster 65,000 BTU beast won't fit in the clearance you have, there's a excellent chance you'll still manage quite nicely with a smaller unit. I believe that many buyers get larger stoves than are really needed. If the layout of your home doesn't allow the heat to distribute evenly, the far end of the house is still going to be chilly whether your stove puts out 35,000 BTUs or 80,000.

Home design will greatly affect how much heat from your stove gets to where you need it. Although I'm not going to get into too much of that because all homes are, and should be, unique, I will share some general thoughts before describing my own installation.

Open designs—wide open rooms, hallways connecting all of the rooms, and open stairwells connecting levels—help the heat to dissipate throughout the house. Rooms on outside walls should generally have their doors open to allow warm air in. Having a central location for the stove itself, perhaps with a center chimney, is great. If you have a centrally located main living area with an outside wall to vent the stove, that can also be a good choice. Even though you may not consider your house very open, air has a way of spreading. One quick test and you can eat the results: cook up some bacon in the kitchen and station someone at the opposite end of the house without telling them why. When you hear them yell "Hey, are you cooking bacon?" that'll tell you that air is really moving around your home, even if you don't feel it. To increase the sensitivity of this test, borrow or rent a teenager if you don't have one of your own.

Another test that's not quite as entertaining: if you have a multi-zone conventional heating system, turn off all but one of the zones on a really cold day for 6 or 8 hours. If the unheated zones stay reasonably warm, you can figure that heated air from the zone that is running is spilling over and mixing into the other zones at a substantial rate. Try out each of the zones in this fashion, and the one that produces the most comfortable temperatures in the other zones is a likely candidate for the best place to have a pellet stove.

Many folks think of a pellet or a wood stove as a "point source" of heat. It's true that the heat from these units originates at a single location. With a furnace, you have radiators, baseboards, or air ducts giving you multiple "hot spots" around the house, as they mechanically deliver the heat where it's wanted. On the other hand, a pellet or wood stove has no octopus of tentacles delivering heat bundles to far-off places in the house. Brings visions of Charles Dickens figures dressed in ratty coats, scarves, and torn fingerless gloves all huddled around a tiny coal grate, doesn't it?

Fortunately, we have our vocabulary word for today: "entrain". Besides "boarding a train", entrain also means "a fluid or current sweeping something along in its flow". If you blow hard through a plume of cigarette smoke, the current of your breath grabs some of the smoke and carries it along, mixing and diluting it. It is the same with pellet stoves—they have a powerful distribution fan, so that extremely hot air blowing out of the stove entrains significant amount of cool room air and mixes with it, creating a much larger volume of warm air. If your house has any sort of air circulation to it, the warm air will start moving all over the house, through open doors, stairwells and hallways. Cool air, being denser, will keep being sucked into the pellet stove since the air intakes are always near the floor. Convection and airflow can move warm air all throughout your home, provided that the air has openings to travel through. It isn't always necessary to have a "heat distribution network" of radiators or ducts to move heat around; your entire house is really just a maze of heating ducts, cleverly disguised as doors, halls, and stairways.

AIRFLOW IS A BIG PART OF DISTRIBUTING YOUR HEAT

Less open layouts can be made to work but clearly take a bit more consideration to get right. In New England, we have many 200-year old farmhouses that just "grew". They tend to have lots of rooms and doors with no clear airflow paths and often long, narrow, and perhaps uninsulated passages connect different parts of the house, not to mention leaky windows and doors. Some rearrangements, such as removing a wall to create a combined living and dining room can help here. Arranging a short section of ductwork through a wall with a small fan can help move warm air to a room that's not "on the path". If you're already committed to pelleting, it's not a bad idea to save any home modifications until you install and try out the stove for a while. We had several rooms we were certain that the pellet stove was not going to heat. Even with our huge wood stove running in years past, we had to run a small electric room heater in our bedroom (upstairs, far end of house) to keep the icicles out of my mustache. So, we were positive that the pellet stove, going into the wood stove's old spot, was obviously not going to heat those rooms quite enough, right? As it turns out, the bedroom is far warmer than it ever was with the wood stove running, and we're planning to get a lighter weight quilt. Know anyone that wants to buy a nice little electric room heater?

A heat-distribution trick that works well for quite a few folks is to use a regular portable air-circulating fan to help move the heat from where it's trapped to where it's wanted. The obvious setup is to put a fan near the stove and try to blow some of the warm air down the hall into the rest of the house. However, a number of folks have reported that it's much more effective to position the fan OUTSIDE of the stove area, and blow cool air INTO the "stove room". The denser, cooler air is much more effective at displacing the lighter, warm air into the rest of the house than trying to force the light, warm air to displace cold, dense air.

In the case of open home layout, the appropriate size of the pellet stove could be quite different, as a great deal of the "heat need" of the home will be handled by the pellet unit. Hence, it would be a good idea to maybe head for the larger end of the range of sizes we targeted earlier, i.e. closer to ½ of the furnace BTU capacity. For the closed and divided-up house design, you may not be able to take advantage of a high heat capacity stove, because the heat just won't get down to the other end without some house remodeling, and the stove will run at only a fraction of its output capacity. A smaller capacity stove that heats only the portion of the house near the stove may make more sense in this case. You might even consider installing two small stove units at opposite ends of the house. One practical consideration is that large capacity stoves tend to have large volume pellet hoppers. This amounts to kind of a lifestyle issue, but if you hate filling the hopper a couple times a day, or if you like to go skiing every weekend in the winter, being able to fill the hopper with enough pellets to last more than a day is a real treat. Some companies even sell hopper-extensions that hold up to three or four bags of pellets, which you can attach when you're leaving for a few days.

I really should mention another means of sizing the stove, based on empirical evidence from other users. Pellets have a certain BTU rating per pound, and most pellets are rated in the neighborhood of 7,500-8,000 BTUs/pound. Given that most pellet stoves are rated at about 85% efficiency, we can estimate that burning a pound of pellets throws around 7,000 BTUs into your living space. With night lows of 10 F to 20 F where I live, I'm burning just under two bags, say 70 pounds, of pellets a day, which is approximately 490,000 BTUs. I can compute my heat loss as being in the neighborhood of 490,000 BTUs/24 hours or around 20,000+ BTUs/hour averaged over the day. As the peak demand is obviously at night, I should add extra for that, and some more for those times it gets down to the minus-single-digits. So I can back-calculate that I should've purchased at least a 35-40,000 BTU/h stove. It confirms what I already have found out from experience that my 50,000 BTU/h stove can provide pretty much all of the heat I could ever use for my home, on the coldest nights in my neck of the woods.

The experience of online users in cyberspace is similar; most report a maximum usage of 1, 1 ½, or 2 bags of pellets a day, depending on climate and the size of their house, which implies that very few, if any, are really utilizing capacity exceeding 40-50,000 BTU/h. Those of you in REALLY chilly places, of course, should add extra capacity. This applies to those of you living in much of Canada or North Dakota, for instance, or those trying to heat an 1820's farmhouse! Those of you in more moderate climates than New England could likely use a somewhat smaller capacity stove and be perfectly happy.

An occasional owner will report that he has an 'X' BTU/hour stove, and it's not big enough! He wishes he'd gotten the "two-times-X capacity" stove, or at least the next model up the line. But if you find out how many pounds of pellets he's going through in a day, it will likely turn out that his stove is not able to distribute all of the heat it's capable of providing due to his home layout. If it's cozy in the stove room, but chilly in a far bedroom, it's likely that the heat just isn't making it that far! A bigger stove is probably not the answer. A 50,000 BTU stove running 24x7 at its rated maximum output should go through at least four bags of pellets a day. So if someone owns a 50,000 BTU stove and says it's not big enough for his house, ask if they're going through about four bags a day—if they are, then their stove REALLY might be too small, or maybe they're trying to heat the Superdome. It's like someone thinking they'll get to their job in downtown rush-hour Manhattan a lot quicker if they just had a Ferrari. Clearly, there are other factors involved. I have nothing against big stoves, but they can be more expensive than what you really need, and may provide very little real advantage. There are only a few days a year that your stove will actually need to reach its maximum possible output.

By now, you're thinking about house designs, placing a stove, how big a size is appropriate, and other stuff. Here's (groan) yet another problem you can run into—Thermostat Wars! No, no, it's not about that wonderful TV sitcom stuff where the husband and wife argue that it's too cold or too hot in the living room with each of them changing the setting every two minutes. Here's what I'm really talking about. We're laying out a house design, with two heating sources in it—your new pellet stove, and your old furnace. Let's imagine doing this as POORLY as we can, just to illustrate the point... I'm going to place the temperature sensor for the pellet stove and the furnace right next to each other, just a few inches apart. Set them to both heat to 70 degrees and watch the fun begin! It's cold in the house now, so both heat sources kick in. After a bit, the temperature gets to 70; the pellet stove decides that it's perfect now, and pretty much shuts down completely.

Meanwhile, the furnace isn't shutting off, because its thermostat will allow it to "swing" up to 72, so it cranks on for a while. Finally, it hits 72, and the furnace shuts down. It'll go back on when it hits 68 again, the low end of its range. The temperature starts to sink with both heat sources off, until we hit 70. Now the pellet stove computer realizes that it has to crank on hard to keep its temperature sensor right on 70. As it does a great job, the temperature is now holding at 70 within a fraction of a degree. So great in fact, that the furnace thermostat right next to it NEVER gets down to 68 again, and the furnace NEVER comes on again. The end of the house that was the responsibility of the furnace to keep warm gets really chilly, because the pellet stove has won the Thermostat War. If you now turned up the furnace thermostat a couple of degrees, it could easily overwhelm the pellet stove and now the pellet stove end of the house would start getting cold, because its sensor is too close to the furnace thermostat. Thermostats are like those nasty little grade school classmates we all had that just didn't Share Well. Probably run with scissors, too.

To avoid this problem, physically separate the controls for your multiple heat sources by some distance. Even then, there can be interaction, but it can in fact be useful when thought out well. In my own home, I have a "furnace zone" of the house, and a "pellet zone". The respective sensors are well apart from each other, but I set the pellet stove desired temperature at about 70-71, and the furnace zone setting about 2-3 degrees lower, at 67 or 68. Because I have a fairly open design house, enough heat "spills over" from the pellet zone into the furnace zone to keep the furnace zone at about 68 degrees, WITHOUT ever having the furnace running at all! The spilled heat keeps the furnace thermostat from turning on, unless the weather gets really cold and windy, in which case, the spilled heat coming from the pellet stove isn't quite enough to keep the thermostat temperature up, and the furnace goes on. So, I have essentially an automated system to heat my home ENTIRELY on pellets, UNLESS it gets really cold, and then the furnace will start to contribute, too. I could also take leave of my senses and turn the furnace thermostat up to 74 or so, in which case the furnace heat would start to spill back to the pellet zone, and the pellet stove would turn off completely, because the heat is being supplied solely by the furnace. As these examples illustrate, it's worthwhile to consider the interactions between your different heat sources and their control mechanisms. If necessary, "fudge" the settings to favor the pellet system. Your wallet will thank you.

If you home has only a single conventional heating zone, adding a pellet stove could cause end up causing "cold spots" if there are distant rooms that rely on some furnace heat, but now the furnace no longer runs. On the other hand, you might end up with some "hot spots" if the furnace still runs occasionally, and both the pellet stove and furnace are dumping heat into a single room. If either of these conditions occurs, you may need to consider moving the thermostat for the furnace, and perhaps shutting down heat registers or bypassing radiators to avoid the "hot spots". Adjust gradually, tweak settings, and these sorts of problems will iron themselves out.

If the Thermostat War seems to be impossible to win, many pellet stoves have a "secret weapon" known as "stove temperature mode". It's kind of disappointing to be thinking about that when I've just gone over how wonderful temperature sensors are, vs. thermostats, but this can be useful in some situations. "Stove temperature mode" just means that the heat output is not controlled by the room's temperature. There's a little dial with numbers from 1 to 10, and you set the amount of heat you want, from candle-flame to erupting volcano. This has the same effect as it would on a wood stove—with a wood stove, you feed small or large amounts of wood, and set the air inlet for a little (low heat output, long burn time) or lots of air (huge amount of heat and burns quickly). Since the pellet stove is now ignoring room temperature, if you set it on "10" and the temperature shoots up to 80, well, it's just going to keep climbing to 90, until you knock it back to "6". Do it in July and you can even create a whole-house sauna.

Why are we messing with this, anyway? Glad you asked. There are circumstances where we may not want the pellet stove to do all of the heating. Especially in a segmented house design with restricted air distribution, we might prefer to have the pellet stove supply only a "base" amount of required heat centrally, while additional heat circulates to outlying rooms via conventional forced-hot-water or forced-air system. With the pellet stove set to deliver a constant heat output, say "5" on the dial, the furnace doesn't have to burn nearly as often, but the heat baseboards or ducts in the distant rooms still get a regular shot of warmth. Distant rooms getting too chilly? Drop the pellet heat setting to "4", and the furnace will run a little bit more. Up to "6", the furnace runs less. A setup like this allows you to continue saving substantially on your oil/propane bill, while avoiding the possibility of Thermostat Wars. And it keeps you from ending up with penguins in your outlying rooms.

Stove temperature mode is also useful if you have a pellet stove installed in an outbuilding, say a garage or workshop, which is normally not heated. It's a cold day, and you want to work in the garage? Set the temperature on "3", and it'll provide just enough warmth to take the chill off. If I used the room temperature sensor in this situation, it would immediately start blasting its maximum heat output in order to get the temperature from 35 up to 70. One nice thing about "stove temperature mode" is that it is very responsive. Turn up the output, or turn it down, and in a few minutes the output stabilizes at the new setting. Now there's something that doesn't work at all on a REAL wood stove.

FOR WOOD STOVE OWNERS

Since many readers are considering a move from an existing wood heat system to a pellet stove, we should have an in-depth comparison between pellet heat and wood heat. Wood heat is very popular in our area of New England, and rightfully so. I've heated my home primarily, even entirely, with wood for more than 20 years, and even after replacing the wood stove with a pellet one, we still have a fireplace that needs a cord or so of wood each year. We have an awful lot of trees here that provide ready fuel, and for some people, this source can be pretty cheap if they are willing to do the work of harvesting the trees, cutting them up, splitting, and using their own firewood. However, even this is not really free, since it involves the occasional new chainsaw or repairs to the old one, perhaps a log splitter, gas and oil, splitting tools, a pickup truck, and a couple tubes of Ben Gay. More commonly in this area, people buy firewood from dealers, typically already split and cut to length, green or dry. Most heating calculators show that the cost of heat from firewood is roughly comparable to the price of pellet heat, although this varies somewhat from year to year. So, are there advantages of pellet heat that would make us choose pellets over using wood heat?

WHERE'S IT ALL GOING?

First, firewood is delivered by a truck, and then dumped in a heap on your driveway or lawn. Four or five cords of wood is an awful lot of wood and makes a huge pile that typically needs to be stacked, which requires hours and hours of bending and lifting. In many cases, at least some of the wood requires additional splitting if the chunks are too large for your wood stove.

Pellets come already stacked and delivered to their final resting spot by forklift. There is no labor involved, and your yard looks neater already! A typical 'dump' of a winter's supply of wood (say, 4 cords) would be approximately 10 to 12 feet wide, and perhaps 25 to 30 feet in length, a minimum of about 300 square feet, where the equivalent in pellets (4 tons) would occupy an 8' by 8' area, 64 square feet, or less than 25% of the space. Note that if you have been heating with wood, and know how much wood you typically use during a season, you should expect to use one or two MORE tons of pellets than the number of cords of wood that you now use. There's a good (and delightful!) reason for this that I'll discuss shortly.

In addition, by its nature, wood tends to be messy, as there is bark, sawdust, leaves, mold, wood chips, dirt and mud, insects, and the occasional skunk or snake that come hand-in-hand with having a woodpile. Not to mention the dirt, sawdust, and bark that will form a path from your side door to the wood stove. Wood ashes swirl out into the room each time you toss a few more sticks into the wood stove. Pellets are different. They tend to be very neat, and are well contained, with only a minor amount of dust distributed when loading the stove. Every week or so, the pellet ashes must be emptied, but this is the only time that they have a chance to escape, and we find that the house is considerably less dusty and gritty during the winter season than it was before.

IT'S THAT TIME OF DAY AGAIN

When comparing wood and pellet systems, let's consider that not-terribly-rare event called 'nighttime'. For years, our evening ritual was to shove every stick that would fit into the wood stove, dial down the air intake for an extended, slow burn time, and head for bed. Invariably, each night, I'd wake up around 3 A.M. and hear the furnace kicking in because the fire had burned low, then argue with myself for a while before (maybe) deciding to go downstairs and stoke the fire again. If I did get up—about a 60/40 odds—the new wood would take a while to get going and finally, by 5 A.M. or so, things would be good again, with the furnace shut down and the wood stove cranking like mad. To recap: with the wood stove scenario, as the heating demand increases (it gets colder as the night goes on), the actual heat output DECREASES, since the wood is burning up and not being re-supplied continually. Hardly ideal. In addition, you lose a lot of sleep tending the stove. Unless you ignore it. Again, not ideal.

Contrast that with how a pellet stove works—as the heating demand increases, the pellet stove computer senses that it's getting colder faster, and INCREASES its heat output! Now there's a concept worth its weight in gold. This leads to a conclusion I mentioned briefly before—you will likely use more pellets than cords of wood, because the additional pellets are replacing the oil or propane that your furnace would have used coming on at 3 A.M. Since, for a given amount of heat, pellets are about 1/4 to 1/3 the cost of oil/propane, each additional bag of pellets you burn saves you a pretty substantial chunk of money. At current local prices for my propane, I think of it this way: for every bag of pellets I shove into my stove, someone is shoving a $10 bill in my pocket. I'm saving that money by NOT burning the equivalent BTUs worth of propane.

When I ran the wood stove in years past, I still ended up with monster propane bills, because I wasn't up every hour during the night to feed the stove, and was at work (and not feeding the stove) during the day. Even considering that I "heated with wood" pretty aggressively for years, the pellet stove is saving me about $1500-

$2000 in propane costs each heating season. Fairly conservatively, I expect the 'payback time' for purchasing and installing a pellet stove in my type of situation to be 2 years, 3 at most. In other parts of the country, and depending on your current mix of heat supply, your payback time will be shorter or longer. Some folks will tell you that converting from wood to pellet heat isn't sensible economically; after all, cordwood and pellets cost about the same per million BTUs, right? Now you know exactly why you should just laugh quietly to yourself when you hear that. If you want a better estimate of the actual cost of wood heat vs. pellet heat, estimate your current price per million BTUs as approximately halfway between the cordwood BTU cost and the propane or oil BTU cost.

I just ran my latest local fuel-cost numbers through the fuel calculator. These vary from year to year, but are still a good way to illustrate a point. A million BTUs of firewood heat by the uncorrected raw calculation was $17.14; $17.71 for pellets, and $58.44 for propane (gulp). Well, burning firewood is still a winner in the raw BTU competition. But considering that I am not always around during the day, or three times a night to feed the wood stove, the furnace still came on a significant part of the day, so my real cost of my hybrid "wood-and-still-a-bunch-of-propane" heat is better estimated at halfway between the propane and wood cost, about $37.79 per million BTUs. It makes the $17.71 per million BTUs for the pellets seem a bit more competitive, doesn't it? Even if you harvest and split your own wood and get it for "free", the hybrid cost of your heat still works out to be $29.22 per million BTUs since you're still using propane or oil. Yes, your "free" firewood heat supply may actually be costing about $12 per million BTUs MORE than buying all of your heat with pellets.

If you're one of those folks who can manage to keep a wood stove going 24 hours a day at the proper heat level and never use your regular furnace at all, then the above doesn't apply. For the rest of us, it's worthwhile considering if we really are saving or actually losing money by sticking with wood.

One thing I was not really expecting when I moved from firewood to pellet heating is that the smoke and smell are pretty much gone. It was rather nice to pull into the driveway and see a curl of smoke coming out of the chimney and smell a bit of wood smoke on a light breeze. Very Norman Rockwell. Of course, the visible smoke and scent are really unburned hydrocarbons and vapor from the water being boiled off of the firewood. With the extremely high combustion efficiency of a modern pellet stove and the low moisture content, most of the hydrocarbons are burned (yielding actual heat) and there is a much smaller amount of water in the exhaust, so you normally don't see any smoke at the chimney except when the stove first starts up. If you are seeing smoke from your pellet stove or smelling it strongly, it may be time to check out the stove, as it can be an indication that something's wrong. And if you do miss the smoke and scent of a good wood fire, get to know someone with a nice fireplace, and drop in on a fine snowy evening clutching a nice bottle of wine. It should yield the desired results.

WHEN IS A POUND NOT A POUND?

Finally, one drawback to either wood or pellet heating is that there is a non-trivial amount of physical effort involved in heating a home with wood in any form. Frankly, it's really easy (physically, anyway) to have the oil or propane guy show up, fill your tank, and leave a bill for $873.68 stuffed in your door jamb. Repeat every three weeks. Done. Oil or propane is really easy heat, except for the effect on your budget. Burning either pellets or wood requires you to carry that fuel from your fuel-pile to the stove, often a couple of times a day.

Since both fuels are made of wood, and there's not a huge difference in percent efficiency between modern appliances of either type, you'd figure that if you have to carry in a 40 pound bag of pellets, you'd also need to carry in about 40 pounds of wood for the same amount of heat, right? Great theory, only it's way wrong. What's up with that? In a word, WATER. In manufacturing, pellets end up having about 2 to 4% moisture content. Green firewood starts out as high as 40%, and even "dry, seasoned" firewood weighs in typically around 20% moisture. So, if you carry in 40 pounds of 'dry, seasoned' firewood, you actually are bringing in 32 pounds of wood and 8 pounds of water. But hold on, it gets worse. In order for wood to burn, the heat of the burning wood must boil off the water content, and that takes a lot of the heat that would otherwise heat your house, converting water to steam and sending it up your chimney. This can be a lot; up to 20% of the wood's heat can be used in just driving off the water. So, from our 40 pounds of firewood, perhaps only 25 actually contributes heat to the house. Here's the bottom line for physical activity: in terms of lugging fuel around, you have to carry almost twice as much firewood (by weight) to get the same amount of heat in your house. In practical terms, my experience is that I have to carry one, maybe two bags of pellets in for a day's heating, instead of 4, 5, or even more trips to the firewood pile. Oh, wait a minute, and where did all that water and steam from the firewood end up? It's busy condensing and making creosote in your chimney, and getting ready for your next big chimney fire. Keep 9-1-1 on your speed dial!

WHAT TYPE OF PELLETS?

There are many different brands of pellets available in the market. In general, the better the quality of pellets that you buy, the more heat you'll get from them. Your stove parts will last longer and the stove will be easier to clean. Many of the companies that produce pellets wholesale their products to a fairly small area—typically a few states—although there are some companies that distribute their pellets regionally or even nationally. As a result, it is likely that the pellet brands I prefer may not be available to you, and vice-versa. It's worthwhile checking into an online forum (see the resource section at the end) to see what people like or don't like in your area. Unfortunately, there is no real way of telling ahead of time how a particular brand of pellet will work in your chosen model of stove— some stoves seem to just 'eat anything', while others are fussier. There are a number of multi-fuel stoves on the market, and they tend to be able to ingest a wide variety of things, including cherry or olive pits, corn, peanut shells, as well as pellets of dubious quality. Even if you intend to run only wood pellets, the multi-fuel stoves may be worth your consideration, especially if you live in an area where there are few brands of pellets available; if the local pellets aren't great quality, having a stove that can digest them well is a real bonus. If you get stuck with a ton of pellets that don't work too well in your stove, don't despair—at least not too much. Some folks like to save these 'stove chow' pellets for 'shoulder season'—spring and fall—when the heating demands are much lower, and burn your best performing pellets when you really need them. You can also experiment with blending the low-grade pellets partially with a higher-grade brand until you finally get rid of them, as this may allow your stove to run more efficiently.

An industry group, the Pellet Fuels Institute, has specified standards for four grades of pellets, namely "Super-Premium", "Premium", "Standard", and "Utility". The primary difference between the grades is ash content, where Super-Premium contains less than 0.5% ash, Premium less than 1%, Standard less than 2%, and Utility less than 6% ash. In addition, the lower grades may contain a higher percentage of moisture (less than 6%, 8%, 8%, and 10%, respectively), which means that you'll get a bit less effective heat, since you need to boil off that water. All grades must meet the same standards for uniform pellet diameter (.25 to .285 inch) and length (less than 1% over 1.5 inches) in order to ensure uniform feeding. In addition, all grades must contain less than 300 parts per million of chlorides, like sodium chloride (salt), which are corrosive to stove parts and chimney. The ash standard is certainly the most important for home users, as ash buildup is the driving factor behind maintenance frequency. Lower moisture content is important as well. There are also PFI standards in several other minor areas, but these are mostly the same or close for all grades and not a concern for the consumer. While four grades of pellets have been defined by PFI, in fact, more than 90% of the pellets produced for general consumer use are PFI Premium grade. Here's the gotcha - manufacturers are not required to get PFI certification, and may, or may not, produce excellent pellets. However, apparently a few non-PFI makers have decided they can call their pellets "premium" even when they would not qualify as such under PFI guidelines. PFI compliant companies should display the PFI seal on their packages, and you should use a certain bit of caution as a consumer before being stuck with a big shipment of sub-standard pellets. As I've indicated, pellet distribution is quite regional, so if there are any questions, a quick note to the online forum may be helpful, being sure to mention where you are located.

WHAT TYPE OF PELLETS?

If you are considering switching to a different brand of pellets (cheaper, not happy with current brand, just want to try something new?) it's worthwhile to give your stove a good cleaning and then buy eight or ten loose bags of the new brand. Run them through your stove, and see if they gum up the works, produce heavy carbon deposits, or gobs of ash and soot. A $25/ton saving can be eaten up very quickly if the new pellets clog up your stove or don't seem to produce as much heat as the higher-priced brand. It's worthwhile noting that many pellet makers will distribute pellets in different packaging through different retailers; some large retail chains and even supermarkets may want their own private store brand on the pellets they sell. These may be the exact same pellets that the company sells through other outlets under its own name, or might turn out to be a different grade of pellet that they produce specifically for private branding. In addition, some makers produce several different formulas of pellet. They may produce both a premium and a super-premium line of pellets, with the latter likely producing more heat and less ash than the premium. Finally, a given manufacturer's pellets may vary slightly from year to year, as different raw material sources are exploited. Whatever your source of pellets, buying them in the spring or summer when demand is lower can often get you a price break of $15 to $30 a ton; and if you've come to really prefer a specific brand, especially one not produced locally, you may find it sold out completely by the time fall rolls around.

When switching pellet brands, a close visual examination of the new pellets is important. They should be reasonably sized, not terribly small and should not be crumbled into little bits. Color may vary widely depending on the species of wood, and is not important. Check how the amount of dust (fines) compares to the old brand. Finding a significant number of pellets that are more than about 1.5

inches long can be a concern, too, as they can "bridge" and block other pellets from entering the feed auger. In daily use, keep one lazy eye on the pellets as you pour them into the stove, as there are rare reports of nails, staples, metal bits, cardboard, and other cool goodies turning up in the bags. It's quite unlikely you'll run across anything, but if you do see something suspicious, yanking it out before it enters the stove can save you an hour or two later of learning how to unstick a jammed feed auger, instead of using the time constructively to put out milk and bake cookies for Santa.

People often wonder if hardwood or softwood pellets are better. Both have proponents and, in addition, many pellet makers offer mixes like 50/50 or 60/40 hard/soft blends. Wood stove owners may have some built-in bias toward hardwood pellets, since a cord of hardwood produces a lot more heat than a cord of pine. But cords of firewood are measured by volume, rather than by weight. It's the old kindergarten riddle—"Is a pound of feathers heavier than a pound of lead?"

Pellets of either soft or hard wood have been compressed to roughly the same density and moisture content, and contain about the same amount of burnable matter, so a ton of hardwood pellets contains a similar heating value to a ton of softwood pellets, and occupies exactly the same storage volume. Some softwood pellets contain a high percentage of resin and pitch, which burn very hot, and may even have a slightly greater heating value than hardwood. Still, this is not always the case and, in some instances, the additional resins and gums may cause more rapid fouling of the stove and chimney. Some brands made of softwood are among the best consumer-rated pellets available, with slightly higher BTU ratings and lower ash output that hardwood equivalents, but much depends on the individual manufacturer, their quality control and raw material suppliers. Many hardwood or mixed hard/soft pellets rate right at the top, also. As with any change, it's a good idea to audition at least a few sample bags before you commit to buying in bulk.

CONTROLS AND WHAT THEY DO

How do you control your pellet stove? If you're used to a wood stove, tweaking a few things to get the right heat output and efficiency comes fairly naturally to you; all you need to do is add more or less fuel, adjust the air supplies, or turn the circulating fan up and down. On the other hand, if you've been a 'thermostat and furnace' person all along, things will take some getting used to. Still, you too can cheer up, as running a pellet stove is easier than running a car. After all, that has controls for A/C, stereo, headlights, power windows, and cruise control, and you've got that pretty well down. The controls aren't a big deal, but some time spent up-front will help a good deal with getting the most out of your new stove. In addition, there are some subtle differences in how the controls work on different models that may make them more convenient to the way you want to operate your system.

Note that it's worthwhile to understand the controls on your particular stove model; they may all operate pretty much alike in day-to-day usage, but there are some very interesting differences than can be very important when it comes to "abnormal" circumstances, such as power outages. You will learn that lighting most stoves manually if the igniter has burned out is really pretty simple. Before deciding on a model, quiz your dealer on these matters! While it's not really important 99% of the time, you want to be able to get your stove churning out some heat for you during the next ice storm! But first, here are some controls that you can find on just about all stoves on the market now.

All of the stoves I know about have some sort of "pellet feed rate" control. This is pretty much a "set-once-and-forget" control. This controls the maximum rate at which pellets will ever feed into the burn chamber, when the stove computer is calling for its maximum heat output. There will be instructions on setting this up in the owner's manual, or the dealer may have already set it for you to a "normal" setting for the pellets you bought. Still, we do care about this. If the feed rate is too high, partially burned pellets may be pushed into the ash receptacle, leading to more smoke and less heat than you should be getting; and if the feed rate is too low, the stove may not deliver the full amount of heat that it is capable of. One time that you may have to specifically look at this setting is when switching pellet brands, as the burn rate of different pellets can differ significantly, and the pellet feed rate can help with the efficiency and heat output you get. Again, once you've set this up in a good range for your brand of pellets, don't mess with it unless you have a really good reason.

Pellet stoves have two separate fans—each of which may have a separate control—one of which regulates the amount of combustion air delivered to the burn chamber. This may be set at the factory, and might not be readily accessible to the user. This fan's rate is varied by the computer depending on the amount of heat being called for, and unless you really think there is a problem, you won't need to care much. On my stove, I can adjust the maximum flow rate but the control is a tiny unlabeled setscrew recessed in a hole on a dark corner of the control panel that you can only get at with a jeweler's screwdriver while chewing a stick of Juicy Fruit and playing a Beatles record backwards. I don't think they want me messing with it! If you do feel the need to fool with this, note the starting setting, ask someone knowledgeable first, adjust in very small increments and observe the results for a while. I've avoided the temptation to muck around with mine so far; it seems that you could really screw up the efficiency of your stove by adjusting this improperly. Just as well there's no knob for it—especially if you have little kids to "help out" by adjusting it for you.

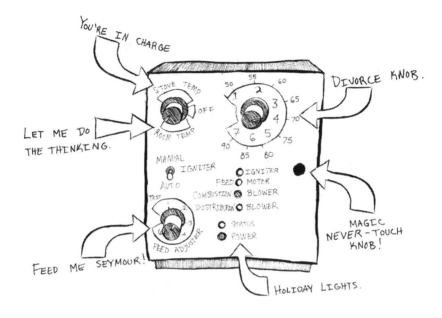

You're in charge

Divorce knob.

Let me do the thinking.

Feed me Seymour!

Magic never-touch knob!

Holiday lights.

STOVE TEMP
OFF
ROOM TEMP
50 55 60
1   2   3 65
4 70
7 6 5 75
90 85 80
MANUAL
IGNITER
AUTO
FEED MOTOR
TEST
COMBUSTION BLOWER
DISTRIBUTION BLOWER
IGNITER
STATUS
POWER
FEED ADJUSTER

TYPICAL CONTROL PANEL AND ITS FUNCTIONS

The second fan is the heat distribution fan. This takes outside (room) air and passes it by the heat exchangers, and then forces the hot air out into the room again. There is typically a dial that controls this process, whereby a higher fan speed rate increases the amount of heat that is captured. Hence, you can set the fan speed lower if the noise is bothersome or when only a small amount of heat is needed, such as a cool fall day. Again, this fan is also controlled by the computer, and if the heat demand is low, the fan may be turned lower than the dial setting, or even switched off.

Most stoves have a dial or two dedicated to setting the desired heat output of the stove. If your stove has a room air temperature sensor, it should also have a temperature dial. Turn the dial to 70, and soon your room will be heated to 70 degrees. Well, maybe. That depends on the placement and calibration of the temperature sensor, airflow around the room, and so on. When I use this mode, I build in a little "mental calibration offset", like some folks that always run their watches 5 minutes fast. In my setup, if I want the room temperature to be 70 degrees, I need to set the temperature dial to around 72 because I didn't place the temperature probe very carefully. In fact, I wouldn't care much if the dial was just numbered from one to ten. I know what dial setting I need to use, and confirm it with a thermometer in the room. If I'm chilly, I crank up a degree from where I was. Some folks prefer to have the dial temperature correspond exactly with the actual room temperature, and this can usually be accomplished after some trial-and error by changing the sensor placement relative to the door, ceiling, window, floor, or stove. The most important part of sensor placement is that it be in a spot where the temperature remains consistent, in other words, not close to an outside door or place that gets a draft.

Many folks prefer NOT to use the room temperature setting, and some stoves do not have a temperature sensor at all. For these stoves, there is a "stove temperature" setting, generally based on an exhaust-temperature probe. Turning to a particular setting on this dial will send a constant amount of heat into the room, regardless of the actual temperature in the house. That dial on my stove doesn't even have numbers; one end is marked "low" and the other end is "high". Other stoves might have a one-to-ten dial. In any case, if your house is too cold (or too hot), give the knob a little twist. In the evening, when it's colder outside, turn it up a smidgen; when you go to bed, turn it down a notch or two. Although just "setting the temperature" using the room temperature dial seems to require the least messing around, many members of the online pellet community prefer to use the stove temperature setting. For one, when using the room temperature setting, the stove noise (fans and auger) may increase or decrease several times an hour depending on the heat demand, and some folks find that to be somewhat annoying. Also, there is some evidence that just setting the stove speed to a constant output is more efficient for the stove, and yields slightly more heat for the same amount of pellets burned. In any case, how you run the stove depends a great deal on the season, weather, stove model controls, your preferences, and even the layout of your home. There's really no right answer for this one. The online forums have a vigorous and lively ongoing debate concerning this subject, and it's worth some experimenting to see what works best in your situation.

OUTSIDE AIR

Here's something that is not exactly a control, but an accessory that controls where your combustion air comes from. It can be added to most stoves if you don't get one at install time, and is referred to as an OAK. We're not talking trees here, but rather referring to an "Outside Air Kit". These provide cold, outside air for the stove to use for combustion, rather than using the nice inside air you just warmed up. Pellet stoves all have sealed forced exhausts, to force all of the combustion products outside. With the exhaust being pushed out, the air in the house is now at a slightly lower pressure than the cold outside air, which starts finding ways to creep in to equalize the pressure, potentially leaving someone's bedroom with a big chill and just maybe someone else sleeping on the sofa. An outside air kit is basically a tube, with a valve that allows air to be sucked from outside the house into the stove's combustion air intake, and some method of keeping out spiders, bats, chipmunks, and California condors that would love to cozy up on your sofa with you. The tube can go through the wall if you have a direct exhaust, or up the same way as the chimney, or even down through your floor and out through a basement wall or window.

There is no real consensus on how useful these kits are; some folks think they're great and wouldn't consider an installation without; others think it's much ado over nothing. In my view, it all depends on where your combustion air comes from if you don't have an OAK—I have a somewhat leaky basement, and my stove is very near the top of the stairs leading down, so the majority of my combustion air seems to be coming "from outside"—via the basement—even without the kit. My windows and doors don't seem to be especially drafty when the stove is on. But, if your stove is in the living room, and you feel drafts coming in when the stove is running, it may be something to consider. In any case, an OAK can be added later if you decide it's worthwhile. I did find an excellent discussion of OAKs that concludes that there is little reason to consider them, and even potential drawbacks and hazards, at http://www.woodheat.org/the-outdoor-air-myth-exposed.html.

Common occurrences such as gusty winds from different directions can influence the drawing power of the OAK, and could even turn it from an air inlet into an air outlet. It's worthwhile to consider this point of view, but I think there are excellent arguments on both sides.

MAD SCIENTISTS?

There are a number of articles on the web regarding interesting stove modifications for the super-dedicated tinkerers out there, including adding 7-day programmable setback thermostats, and even remote control of your pellet stove via Internet. Some of these modifications are actually pretty simple, and may be just the ticket for getting your stove to work the exact way you prefer. If you think that you want to do that kind of thing, check online, as the procedures usually involve bypassing or spoofing the existing controls. For instance, some folks developed circuits to electronically modify resistance in the room temperature sensor, which allowed them to computerize the stove's temperature setback schedule by faking the stove's computer into thinking the temperature was either higher or lower than the actual room temperature. Such modifications are extremely manufacturer and stove model-specific, and may cause problems with your warranty.

USING MANUAL IGNITION

One last control that all stoves with automatic ignition should have is an "automatic/manual" toggle switch. When set to "automatic", if you turn on the stove, pellets will begin to be fed into the burn pot, and an electric igniter will be fired up, lighting the pellets within a couple of minutes. Once the pellets are burning, the igniter shuts off. If the stove is in room temperature mode, and the stove shuts off completely, the ignition cycle will repeat whenever heat is called for again. This is quite convenient, and many folks use their stoves in this manner. However, there are problems you may encounter. First, the igniter really sucks a fair bit of electricity. It's an electrical heating appliance all by itself, and may draw power in excess of 400-500 Watt when the igniter is running. If you are running room temperature mode on a cool spring day, the stove may turn on or off a couple of times an hour, with each cycle running a 500 W heating element for 5 minutes or so. Second, the igniters have a finite life span; so, the more you run it, the sooner you'll need to replace it. This is not such a big problem in the prime winter heating season, as the pellet stove would almost never shut down completely, and so the igniter is only running once every couple of days or even once a week after cleaning.

When in "manual" mode, or if you have an older stove or one of the few current non-auto models, the stove will not light itself from a cold state. Switching the stove "on" starts the pellet feed on most stoves, but doesn't ignite the stove. You have to light the pellets manually, using a fire-starter cube or wood shavings to get the initial flame going. Some folks prefer keeping a small plumber's propane torch handy to ignite the pellets. They light pretty readily; I recall camping with the Boy Scouts many years back, and lighting fires – successfully - with wood that had been out in driving rain for several days. Nice, dry pellets are a piece o' cake.

IMPORTANT: for safety, you must NEVER use gasoline, camp-stove (Coleman) fuel, kerosene, lamp oil, rubbing alcohol, paint thinner, or other highly volatile fuel to start your stove, as they can cause all the usual side effects—explosion, severe burns, house fires, and/or death. Just don't do it! Keep the explosive and highly flammable stuff away. Some stove shops sell bottles of "fire gel", which is sort of a jellied alcohol suspension for lighting wood fires or pellet stoves. There are a few reports of folks pouring the fire gel into pellet or wood stoves that still have embers going, and having the bottles burst spilling flaming jellied alcohol, so I would recommend extreme caution when using fire gel, or skipping it entirely and using a wax-based fire cube or similar. Anyway, once started in manual mode, the pellet feed and computer will keep the fire going indefinitely.

Anyway, manual mode lighting is not that daunting; it takes a minute or two, but it's easy. If you are experiencing a power outage, you may want to switch over to manual mode immediately anyway; if you're running off a battery backup or your car's cigarette lighter, running the automatic igniter will really draw down your battery, or possibly damage the inverter connected to the car.

One really interesting difference in stove models pertains to some brands that run their motors internally on 12 volts instead of our usual 110 volts, with an internal transformer converting the wall-outlet power. These stoves can run directly from a 12 volt battery backup, without converting to 110 V. It's an excellent design, and works very efficiently, but the 12 volts will NOT be sufficient to run the automatic igniter on most models. If you have one of these models, you will have to know how to start the stove manually, and should have fire-cubes or other kindling on hand just for that situation. If you have to run your stove from a car (cigarette lighter) inverter, you should also start and run in manual mode. Even stoves that have a 110 V battery/inverter backup system should be lit in manual mode, just to conserve limited battery power. Ask your dealer how the stove you're thinking of can be started in a power-out situation, and what optional accessories he has to make this process easier.

OK, it's manual mode. The power is out, but we've started up the stove using battery backup and a fire cube. What do we expect now? Is the stove going to keep running, or do I have to sleep down here and re-light it once an hour? Here's where it gets interesting: when in manual mode, most stoves will NOT shut down and let the fire go out completely. Even if the room temperature mode tells the computer "it's warm enough in here!" the computer realizes that if it shuts down completely, it will have to be manually restarted. In that case, instead of shutting off completely, it will reduce the feed rate to maintain a very low "maintenance burn", producing only very little heat, but still ready to ignite fully once heat is required again. This saves both electricity and wear-cycles on the igniter, and can help to postpone igniter replacement day significantly.

Still, maybe you're thinking that that automatic ignition thing is pretty darn handy, and you don't want to mess with manual mode, fire-starter cubes, and angry peasants with propane torches? I'm with you there. But, it's incredibly easy to have the best of both worlds. If I need to start up my stove (hey, I just did my weekly quick cleaning), I flip the little toggle switch to "automatic", then switch the dial to call for heat, either with the room temperature setting, or stove temperature mode. In a couple of minutes, the igniter has done its job, and the pellets are starting to blaze; now I flip the toggle switch back to "manual" and I'm done for the week, with the exception of having to haul bags of pellets. The stove will remain burning in "maintenance mode", and never shut off completely. Next week, when it's time to clean, I'll shut the stove to OFF, clean, flip the igniter toggle back to "automatic", and repeat. I don't need to mess with lighting the stove manually, and still manage to save electricity and wear and tear on the igniter.

One last "control" worth mentioning is that most stoves have a pellet-level sensor of some sort. It's not something you see or adjust directly. This tells the computer one simple thing: the stove is out of pellets, so please shut down gracefully and don't sit there spinning the feed auger in an empty hopper. It also leaves a handful of pellets "in the pipeline" so that it can restart promptly. Because of this feature, modern pellet stoves can run out of pellets with no risk of damage, so you can leave the stove running with a full hopper of pellets when you leave for a weekend, and not worry what will happen when it runs out Sunday morning. Similar to your car running out of gas, none of the models I know of will restart automatically when you dump in more fuel, but we've seen that it's just a matter of flipping a switch or two to get it running again.

OTHER STUFF YOU (MIGHT?) NEED

Well, as it turns out, getting a pellet stove and starting off on this endeavor involves not just the cost of a stove and a ton of pellets. There are additional expenditures for things you WILL need eventually; some are sooner (or NOW), and some can be put off more or less indefinitely. Here's at least a list to start with. The peculiarity of your installation and the way you choose to operate your stove will determine the additional things you'll need. Here are some things to think about for the planning budget...

First, it's not a concern where I live, but your town may require a permit or inspections of some kind to install a stove. Check with the town, or your local dealer, as they'll know the applicable regulations. Most places don't have any regulations to worry about, but it's better to know about it up front and pay the $20 than get stuck with a fine.

Installation itself is a pretty minor expense. Or Maybe Not. Many installations can be performed by a decent DIY'er with fairly basic tools, depending on where you plan to vent the stove, and how your installation will conform to your local building code. A simple through-the-wall vent can be pretty easy to install and can usually be done in a few hours with an average set of tools, plus the necessary pipe and fittings to match your stove. For those of you with more thumbs than fingers, a relatively simple, standard installation can be done by your dealer, and will probably run to 200 or 300 dollars. However, if you are tying in to an existing chimney system—an unused fireplace, or your wood stove location—things can get a bit hairy. Old chimney flues can require relining to meet building codes, or could be fine as they are. In any case, the dealer installing your stove should come over and give the planned installation a good examination, inspect the chimney, and so on, BEFORE you commit to buying a stove. Relining the chimney, special piping, or other modifications may be needed to provide adequate clearance. As meeting code standards could end up costing from $500 to well over $2000, it's important to understand the costs and get a firm installation price before you dive into the project.

Many zoning ordinances require or recommend that wood heating appliances have a fireproof hearth pad installed under them. If you have a tile, stone, or concrete floor this could be waived. Regardless of zoning, they are an excellent investment as they protect your floor from the weight of the stove, and can be decorative as well. They are essential for installation on any type of floor that is not fireproof, such as hardwood or linoleum. They can range from simple metal "stove boards" for $75 and up, to decorative tile accent pieces that can cost $300-500 or more. Check with your dealer to ensure that you get the pad that is the proper size for your stove, extending out at least a few inches on all sides. Some of these pads can also be used vertically to reduce the required clearance to walls if your space is not quite large enough.

Cleaning tools are another expense. You can usually make do with tools you already own for quite some time, but eventually you might want a good ash vacuum ($150-$250), chimney cleaning tools (around $100), or even a leaf blower and some fittings. Yes, some folks have figured out how to hook up leaf blowers (the kind with both vacuum and blower ports) to help with cleaning your stove. Some nice videos on YouTube show some folks power cleaning their stove chimneys with leaf blowers, by blowing air out the exhaust port! If you're on a tight budget, you can certainly run your stove with a very minimal set of cleaning tools for a while; a paintbrush, dustpan, scraper, cookie sheet, and a couple borrowed kitchen utensils will give you great bang for the buck.

Pellet storage is another area where you can cheap out or go wacky. Getting a heavy-duty tarp to cover your outdoor pellets is cheap insurance, and the absolute least you should do to prevent fuel damage by the weather. The heavier-weight ones are a better investment here, because they tend to last more than just a season or two, and hang together better when they get laden with 15 inches of half-frozen snow and three corners are frozen down to the driveway. Some folks have built small lean-tos, carports, or sheds to store pellets; these are great because you don't have to shovel and chip a bunch of ice and snow off the top of your pellet pile. Another storage option is to build a rack along your garage wall, which will provide a ton or so worth of dry indoor storage for a minimal cost. Finally, there are various pellet bin designs on the market, ranging from simple reinforced bags with a frame holding a ton or more of loose pellets, to large rigid plastic or metal storage bins that can hold up to five or more tons of bulk pellets. The bulk bins are especially useful for people that may not have the stamina to carry the typical 40-pound bags of pellets. You can fill a smaller bucket from a spout on some of these bins if that is more suited to your personal carrying capability.

Backup power is an area where you may wish to invest. Pellet stoves absolutely require electric power, which is a concern especially to those switching over from wood heat. In one of the big ice storms a few years back, our house was out of power for 13 days. We had a wood stove then, and it saved our cookies, since it required no power (I did get a lot more heat out of it under normal conditions with its distribution blower going, though). During that time, I did end up getting a generator to power the house. A whole-house generator with installation and automatic start and switchover can cost a couple thousand dollars (or way more), but to run a pellet stove and a few lights you may want to consider a smaller, cheaper, portable generator—the type construction workers take to a house they're building to power a radio, Skil saw, and other job site tools. Something rated between 1,000 and 2,000 Watt should be more than enough to run your pellet stove for a few hours a day and they start at only a couple hundred bucks. Another power strategy involves using a battery backup or a "UPS"—an uninterruptible power system. A full inverter backup system, with a heavy-duty deep-cycle marine battery, will probably cost $300 to $400, but will be capable of running the stove for 12 to 18 hours or more, and can be recharged after that time at a friend's house or your office if they are still "on the grid". You can likely keep your house reasonably comfortable indefinitely if you have a place to recharge the backup battery. There are also smaller UPS systems designed for use with computers. They can keep your stove running through brief outages and "power blinks", but are not really well suited to extended outages.

While we're talking power, some sort of surge protector is great insurance for your stove's electrical components. You can get them for $20 to $50; although models are available for less, these typically last only a short time before failing and leaving you unprotected. Try to get a decent quality one, with a protection rating of at least 2,000 – 3,000 Joules or more. Some models even refuse to give power to your appliances if their protection circuits have failed. While this seems like an annoyance, it's better to know that the protection has failed rather than finding out in the next big electrical storm that the power surges are coming straight through a failed unit. They can save the on-board computer on your pellet stove and its other components from being toasted by power spikes and even near-misses by lightning.

Some stove models also have a variety of accessories available, from warming racks for mittens and brass or nickel decorative trim kits, to extended-capacity hoppers. I'd love to have one of those hoppers when I go out of town for a long weekend; my stove could run for several days before the furnace would have to kick in. Alas, I don't think they make one for my particular model, although the standard hopper capacity on mine is around 60+ pounds, about 1 ½ bags.

A recent item I came across is the "pellet basket"—a welded steel basket about the size of a loaf of bread that will hold 10 or 15 pounds of pellets. The steel rods that make up the unit are placed very close together, so that pellets can't escape but air can get in. The basket can be inserted either into the firebox of a conventional wood stove—instead of logs—or, if you don't have logs, in a fireplace, allowing you to burn pellets for a fire during a romantic evening. It doesn't use electricity, so it will definitely run during a power outage! The fire doesn't have the forced air supply of a pellet stove, and although I'd be concerned about how efficiently the pellets would burn, I don't know of anyone who has used one to get further information. I suppose that it fills a small niche in the market, but I think it's more of a novelty for most of us. Still, I've got a big curious streak in me, and would love to see one in operation someday.

One category of machinery that will be of interest to only a very small number of you is your own pellet-making setup. I mention this primarily because people have asked me about it. There's a desire many of us have to use 'free' raw materials we have on hand, and it does sound pretty good, but there are a number of gotchas. First of all, unless you have a commercial operation of some type, having a reliable source of feedstock for making pellets is a concern. That great big brush pile may yield a ton or so of pellets, but that barely gets you a start on this year's supply, and the savings on a couple of tons won't pay for the equipment you need. You are going to need to be good friends with someone that owns a sawmill. Second, consumer pellet mills don't come cheap. Several companies produce pellet mills for the home market, powered by electricity, diesel or a tractor's power takeoff. If you have a source of considerable quantity of sawdust from wood-working or timber operations, you might consider this option, but even the smallest mills available start around $3,000 and up. You can also make your own pellets from grass, nut shells, scrap wood, cardboard, and brush, but these usually require a separate hammer mill to grind the raw material to a usable size, which will add several thousand dollars to the setup cost, and you may also require a drier to reduce the moisture content of the feed material.

Getting set up to produce your own pellets could easily cost upwards of $10,000, which would buy you eight or ten years' worth of commercial pellets for an average home, even before factoring the time to run the mill and the cost of harvesting and hauling the materials. However, if you run a large operation, such as a farm that requires heating several outbuildings and barns, you could end up making this work economically. If you run a lumber mill and have lots of waste sawdust, you could produce enough to generate some extra income. Even the smallest pellet mills have a production capacity that far outstrips the heating requirement of an average household, most with a capacity of 100+ pounds an hour. Even considering time gathering material and running it through the preparation steps, most small mills can produce 10 to 20 bags worth of pellets a day in full swing, much more than the average home can use. The final thing to consider is that the pellets you produce yourself may be of inferior quality to those produced in a large commercial facility, so that even if several of your friends have said they'd buy pellets from you, they may shy away if the pellets don't perform well and burn cleanly in their stoves and furnaces. Although rolling your own pellets may work out for a few of you, most of us will need to rely on commercial pelleting operations. Those who feel the need to be completely independent for their heating needs would do well to stick with the old standby, the wood stove or furnace.

Maintaining Your Stove

Cleaning is a very important part of pellet stove ownership. Since they are somewhat complex pieces of machinery and generate smoke and ash, they require regular tending. Your exact cleaning schedule will depend on your stove design, and type and amount of pellets burned. In general, during the real heating season you should do a "quick clean" around once a week. This will require you to take out ash, brush fly ash off of the heat exchangers to ensure your heat is getting into the house, scrape down carbon buildup on your burn assembly, and clean the sensors that the computer uses to monitor the stove's operation. On a monthly basis, or after burning each ton of pellets, a more thorough cleaning is in order—possibly involving removing plates to clean the igniter assembly and reach some of the inaccessible areas of the stove for a vacuuming. Your owner's manual will give you a good idea what is involved, and when shopping for a stove, have the dealer demonstrate the procedure. Two brands of stoves with similar heat output may require very different cleaning efforts. During the summer, you may want to have the stove dealer or chimney service that's familiar with pellet stoves come out and inspect the stove and chimney to ensure that things are operating safely, and at peak efficiency. Although pellet stoves produce a much smaller quantity of creosote than wood stoves, periodic chimney inspections are still important. Some brands of pellets and stove designs may tend to produce much more creosote than others, although very few pellet users I've run across have had any serious buildup.

Tools you can use for cleaning include some very basic ones—a 2 or 3 inch wide natural bristle paint brush (nylon bristles melt if the stove is still hot!) for removing ash from heat exchangers, a long handled soft-bristle brush for dusting off sensors, and some type of metal scraper for the burn pot. An old cookie sheet, or an old towel, is nice to put under the stove before you open it up, as there's always some ash clinging to the door that will otherwise fall on the kitchen floor. If your burn pot has holes for combustion air, they can get clogged. I found that a one-inch machine bolt a bit smaller than the holes' diameter will ream them clean quite effectively. While most stoves have an air-wash system to keep their front glass clean, the windows do smoke up after a while and you can clean the glass once the stove has cooled with paper towels and spray glass cleaner.

Most importantly—dispose of ash safely! Hot coals can smolder for a long time and ignite paper or plastic, so must never, ever be placed in your normal household trash container. Place ashes in a fireproof container with lid, such as a small galvanized metal trash can, and leave it outside on bricks for a day or two to ensure that it is completely cool. You can work small amounts of ash into your garden or compost pile and, in the winter, I sometimes just spread the ash thinly on a handy snowdrift in the woods. Always use care with spreading ash outside, especially if there is no snow and the woods are dry; if it's still above freezing you can even spray down the ash with your garden hose.

Other cleaning tools you may want to consider include various types of brushes for the exhaust pipes and chimney. These tools are a great investment if you are a do-it-yourself type, as they can save you the cost of annual chimney cleaning ($150+ around my area). Another excellent investment, in terms of time saved and safety is an ash vacuum. The very fine ash that is produced by pellet stoves can easily wreck a household vacuum or even a shop-vac with frequent use, and the filters on those vacuums are often too coarse to catch all of the dust, which will leave your house enveloped in a bad-smelling smoky ash-cloud. In addition, in terms of safety, inhaling live embbeers into a standard vacuum can cause it to catch fire, either immediately or—even worse—many hours later.

BE CAREFUL WHEN USING A REVERSIBLE VACUUM!

The best ash vacuums—and the only ones you should even consider—have fireproof metal containers and fire-resistant filters, so that sucking up the occasional live coal won't burn your house down. Be extremely cautious when looking online for ash vacuums, as some are NOT fireproof, and are rated for "cool ash only". These are a dangerous joke. A proper "warm ash capable" vacuum costs perhaps $50 more than the "cool" vacuums, but may save your home and your life someday. Ash insulates live coals extremely well. There have been reports of fires caused by vacuuming up ash in a shop-vac, or disposal of supposedly 'cool' ashes in the household trash, even 12 to 20 hours after the stove has been shut down. Ash should always be disposed of in a fireproof metal container and left in the container to cool for at least a day or two before exposing it to anything remotely flammable.

There are many different ways to clean stoves, some quite ingenious and laborsaving, that may depend on your exact style of installation. Specifics of your stove design will be described in your owner's manual, and your dealer should be able to demonstrate how you particular model should be cleaned. Looking up information online on particular cleaning problems, or ideas for maintenance of your particular stove model, is also well worth investing an hour or two of your spare time.

PLANNING FOR INSTALLATION

The next few sections delve into the considerations relevant when planning your installation. We'll cover some possible issues with the authorities, considerations on placement, stove features to consider when shopping for your stove, pellet storage options, pellet types, and offer some help in estimating the size of stove that will fit your needs. Our first order of business: Ya Got's Ta Deal with Th' Man!!!!

CHEESE IT! THE COPS!

Well, to be fair, you really aren't likely to get busted for installing a contraband pellet stove. However, institutional challenges and regulations could be among the most difficult things to sort out. This includes rules, regulations, covenants, zoning, and so on. Let's see what issues may arise. First, it is somewhat common for entire communities to be subject to zoning regulations and ordinances—likely dating back many years—banning wood-burning appliances of any type in order to reduce smog formation. Pellet stoves burn far more cleanly than conventional wood stoves and some communities now offer exemptions for pellet stoves; if not, you may be able to apply for a variance with your Zoning Board, or building inspector. I would strongly advise to check with them first, as a few phone calls may save you a whole stack of grief later.

Another "gotcha" for some were condominium association rules and neighborhood covenants. Again, if you belong to a condominium or community association that disallows them, there may be a variance procedure, and sometimes you can work with the committees to recommend an update to the rules—after all, pellet stoves actually do make much better neighbors than wood stoves.

However, condominiums and apartments (as well as dense urban areas) may be unsuitable for pellet ownership for a variety of reasons. Exhaust from your stove may infiltrate your neighbors' apartment or home, and often you have no good place to store pellets.

Finally, there's one area where it may be advantageous to, shall we say, embellish the truth a bit—dealing with your homeowner's insurance company. If you apply for new insurance, or go through a policy review, they usually ask about your "primary home heating system". Some companies will instantly shred your application if you tell them that you primarily heat your home with "wood" or "wood pellets". They don't regard wood-burning as a proper first-line heating source; one possible justification being that if you go away for a week, they figure that all your pipes are gonna freeze, and they will be required to issue a good sized check, paying for a plumber and your flooded basement. In addition, if you bail on your mortgage, they foresee having a hard time selling a house that has "wood stove" as the main heat source.

However, most of us aren't going to toss our old oil-burner furnace out on the heap just to replace it with a wood or pellet stove; even if we hope to get most of our actual heat from burning pellets. The 'conventional' system is still viable if we're away on vacation, or the pellet stove needs a repair. So, when the question comes up, tell the insurance company your "primary heating system" is "propane forced hot water" or "electric baseboard" or whatever. Say it Loud and Proud! Then go home and burn some pellets in your incense burner, as penance for fibbing to the Insurance Gods.

Special note here: although this book does not go deeply into "pellet furnace/boilers" that would actually COMPLETELY replace your oil or gas furnace, it may be a very real concern with getting insurance because some companies simply refuse to accept pellets as a primary heat source. Check with your insurance company, and if need be, with the insurance company you're about to switch to, to ensure they'll cover you.

INSTALLATION DAY

My goodness. You went ahead and ordered a stove, and now it's really showing up. Wow! The big day has arrived! The new stove is showing up on your doorstep, with a couple of guys from the dealer all ready to haul the new appliance in, and (maybe) your old wood stove out. My dealer came with a battery-powered, motorized hand-truck to haul the stove up the stairs; seeing that was nearly worth the price of admission by itself. As I looked at that gadget, I remembered all of the wood-stoves, desks, mattresses, sofas, flotsam, jetsam, and other heavy junk I've carried up and down those stairs over the years. Santa??? Not too likely, but a feller can dream, can't he...? Anyway, back on subject. Installation day is going to be your best chance to have your dealer on-site and checking out your installation for you. Skip checking out Facebook and texting your buddies for an hour or two. Watch the guys like a hawk, and ask as many questions as you can come up with. If you see something that looks sloppy or unsafe, ask them about it, and make them sort it out TODAY. Even if it's August, have them fire up the stove and adjust the feed and fan to their optimum settings. Have them run over the controls and explain how each one functions. Ask them to show you the cleaning procedure – again - even though you saw it at the dealer's showroom, and see what assemblies you can get at, panels you need to remove for annual cleaning and so on. Ask if that 'little noise' you hear is normal. A whole bunch of show-and-tell now might be a big help in the future. Ask about brands of pellets. Anything you can think of is open for discussion on the day of installation. If you have any questions, today is the day you can get them answered, with the dealer on location and looking at your EXACT stove in its EXACT new spot. If you have questions next week, it's not as good. Unless you're having a real problem, they're not likely to come out again until annual maintenance time, and if you go to their shop to ask about adjusting or cleaning, they may not have your exact model set up to show you. So, today is your day. Go nuts; ask all the questions you can think of, even if you asked them before when you were shopping for the stove. In short, your mission today is to be a royal pain in someone's buttsky. You'll be glad you did.

Back to the Budget

So, at this point, we're perhaps thinking that a pellet stove is going to save us some money in the fairly near term. Boy, in the dead of winter, this is going to be a real utility-bill-killer, eh? Well, to be fair, that is when you use the most heat, and certainly a great time to have the pellets roaring 24/7. However, it's time to mention a concept that most of you know pretty well, but may have rarely, if ever, seen described in print—the Shoulder Seasons. For us folk up north, that starts around the end of September, possibly early October, and is heralded by folks that, on seeing each other in the coffee shop or diner downtown, start greeting each other with "Hey, John, it was down to 34 at my place last night—turned on your heat yet?" There's something about the prospect of having your pocket sucked dry by the oil delivery folks for the next seven months that has people more than willing to endure a little (or lot) of discomfort and chilly evenings before they give in and flip the furnace on. In my neck of the woods, October and November are the months when you need to drag out the flannel shirts and sweaters just to *endure* being in your own home in the evening. By the first of December or so, even the REAL die-hards have cracked, and have finally resigned themselves to the oil bills and flipped on the thermostat.

But, wait! That's not YOU I'm talking about, because YOU have a wood stove, right? Well, as it turns out, Shoulder Season is even WORSE, in some ways, for wood stove owners. Here's why: the wood stove won't light itself, and it won't shut itself off! In the dead of winter, a regular old wood stove is a pretty darn nice thing. You start it up, you feed it a few times a day, get it roaring-blistering hot, and it's cranking a ton-o-heat as long as you keep it fed. I've run my own wood stove continuously without lighting a second match for 60 days or more. But in Shoulder Season, you don't want the stove going all day—good grief, it's 66 degrees and sunny at noon! So, in the morning you have to let it die out, because if you run it all day, the house'll heat up to 86 degrees, and you'll feel like you're in the boiler room of the African Queen. Late that evening, it's dropped to 36 again, the cat's curling up to you closer than a three-dollar tattoo, and you decide it's time to start gathering kindling, wood, and huffing and puffing to light the stove AGAIN—20 to 30 minutes to make sure it's caught on and running right. So a wood stove owner may light his stove once in December, once in January, but in October he might light it TWENTY times. Having done this dance for several decades myself, I can tell you that it's a big time-sink to keep gathering kindling and paper, laying the fire, and lighting the stove every day. It's really easy to just blow it off, get a glass of Scotch and a good book, and crank on the furnace for a few days, or a week or two. Lazy, I s'pose? You bet. Still, I'd wager more than a few of you have gone that route at least a few times, eh?

The point—finally!—is that if you have a wood stove, your biggest oil or propane bills might NOT be in January or February when your wood stove is cranking hard 24x7, but in October and November, when it's just way easier to flip on the thermostat. There's a Shoulder Season in March and April too, when keeping the wood stove going and re-lighting every day gets to be too much bother, and we may just resort to Mother Oil again.

That brings us back around to the pellet stove. Remember, our objection to heating with oil/gas in Shoulder Season (or any time) is that it's Really Expensive, and our objection to heating with wood in spring and fall is that it's a Huge Pain. So, if I suggested that you could heat at the same cost as with wood, and enjoy almost the same convenience as you did with oil, would that be of interest? Well, dear friends, Yes Indeed. From our earlier discussion, you might recall that pellets give about the same amount of heat as the equivalent cost of wood. In addition, the temperature control and automatic ignition on a pellet stove mean that it will LIGHT ITSELF in the evening when it starts getting chilly, and TURN ITSELF OFF in the morning if it warms up outside. No huffing, puffing, gathering kindling, drizzling junk paper with kerosene, candle wax, or bacon fat. Just dump a bag of pellets in every couple days, and enjoy a perfectly comfortable house for that whole season. For about the same cost as wood stove heat, you can get additional 2, 3, or even 4 months *Every Year* of Comfortable Living, in your own home!

One important consideration during Shoulder Season is psychological. Nobody likes throwing on the furnace first thing in the fall, because you likely have no idea how much it costs! The oil guy comes around to fill your tank every month or six weeks, so you get no gut feeling for how much oil or propane you use on a given autumn night. See if you've got this number on the tip of your tongue: How much does the oil cost to heat your house for one fall night when it gets to 40 degrees overnight? Is it one dollar? Ten? Five? Fifteen? You likely don't have even a rough idea. Then pose the same question to the guy with the pellet stove. He carried in the pellets and knows that the bag lasted about three days in that weather. Based on the cost of a bag of pellets, heating the house for that evening was about $1.70, plus or minus a dime. Knowing what you're shelling out for heat means that you can understand your budget a bit better. It doesn't seem so bad to light up the pellet stove when you know you'll be cozy that evening for the price of a cup of crummy fast-food coffee or a small bag of French fries. Don't like fast-food-chain coffee (Um, yeah, that's me!!)? Cup o' decent Joe from most places cost about the same as two days of pellet heat during Shoulder Season. October? Turn on the pellets. It's not costing you much, and you can feel sort of human in your own home for a change.

Another fabulous thing about pellet stoves is how nice it is to get away from them. That's a nice week's February vacation in Sint Maarten I'm referring to! Leave the snowdrifts and 5 degree nights to the stay-at-home crowd. When I had a wood stove, however, it really didn't work out perfectly. A wood stove really will not run by itself for long, and soon the sound of plumbers fixing frozen pipes would be heard through the land. So, I would just have to leave the furnace going with the thermostat down, and face the propane bill when I get back. Most pet-tenders or house sitters are not going to fool around with starting and tending the wood fire every few hours all week! But with the pellet stove, you can show them how to load a bag of pellets once a day, and flip the switch to re-light the stove if it's gone out, and a significant part of your heat use during your vacation can be handled by the pellets. It certainly takes away a little bit of the post-vacation "sticker shock".

SAFETY (A.K.A. BOREDOM)

With any heating appliance, eventually, the subject of safety comes up. There are a number of aspects to consider when heating your home using a pellet stove. Fuel storage is an important one. Pellets aren't liquid or gas, so if their container springs a leak, they're about as exciting as watching grass grow. Sweep them up with a whiskbroom and you're done. Don't need the fire department, or evacuating a three block radius. Well, that was an adventure. Of sorts. What would happen if a loose pellet or two rolls near a source of ignition—the stove, a candle, a cigarette? Well, it will not be quite as exciting as a trickle of heating oil or mist of escaping propane, that's for sure. Pellets are about as safe as a fuel can be when it comes to storage. Even when I used firewood, I managed to get myself stung by a yellow jacket in the woodpile every year or two. No bees or boa constrictors (so far!) in the pellet stacks.

GETTING THERE

Transportation is safer, too. Every year around here, we have a few big oil, gasoline or propane tankers crash, leading to road closures, neighborhood evacuations, infernos, possibly fatalities, and guys running around in HAZMAT suits cleaning things up for days. Transportation of pellets is far safer; if they spill, they just lie there, completely inert. I guess the real danger is that if you let spilled pellets lie out in the rain long enough, they might grow a crop of poisonous mushrooms.

As for the heating appliances themselves, conventional heating systems have excellent safety records when maintained well, and you're likely to continue having one of those around even if you do get a pellet stove. However, there are some real safety differences between wood and pellet stoves if you're switching.

BIG VS. LITTLE

First, there's a big difference in what's going on inside. A modern wood stove at full output has a load of maybe 30 to 50 pounds of wood burning at a relatively slow rate. If you let it just it "go out" without adding more wood, the wood can continue to burn for 8, 10, or even 12 hours, and I've been able to relight my wood stove from the embers even after 24 hours. In a pellet stove, the amount that is burning at any one time is maybe 1 or 2 OUNCES of wood—about a good fistful—and it's burning at a FURIOUS rate. It requires CONSTANTLY feeding pellets and combustion air to keep going, and will go out in less than 15 minutes if the fuel supply stops. Because the wood stove has a massive fire going inside, the entire outside surface of a wood stove is dangerously hot. You can burn your hands or turn water to steam on any external surface when it's really going. Got kids or elderly? Keep them away! A jacket that you've got drying falls over on a wood stove—got 9-1-1 on your speed dial, and a fire extinguisher handy? With a pellet stove, you've got a pretty dinky, wimpy little fire going, and just about all of the heat is getting sucked up by the internal heat exchangers and blown into the room. With many models, the outside surfaces (except for the front glass) are cool enough that you could lean on them for several minutes at a time (trust me on that, I have). Mine is running at full blast right now, and the side and top of the stove measure about 110 F, but the temperature of the front glass and firebox door exceeds 250 F—the only spots you need to avoid touching. One pellet dealer tells me of customers' cats that sleep on top of their pellet stoves. Might even be a good spot to let bread rise.

PELLET STOVES ARE DAINTIER DINERS THAN WOOD STOVES

Even the exhaust flue on mine can be held in my bare hand comfortably unless it's cranking out at maximum (152 F right now, too warm to hold for long, but not likely to cause an instant burn, as would my old wood stove flue, which was often hotter than 400 F). Check with your dealer or visit a friend that has the model you are considering, as the sides and top of some stoves can definitely get much hotter than mine does. I'm very happy not having the possibility of a dangerous burn if someone slips and falls against the stove, or having something catch fire if the kids throw a jacket on top.

Another benefit of the little vs. big fire is that feeding the stove is a lot friendlier. When I would feed my old wood stove, I would open up a cast-iron door (measuring at about 400+ F) into the firebox and shove in wood chunks wearing heavy leather elbow-length gloves and using iron pokers and rakes. While I do this, flaming hot coals are trying to roll out the door and across the floor to find something flammable. This is entertaining for me, but then, I'm a rock-and-ice climber and mountain biker, so a little bit of really wacky junk is OK. I'm pretty handy at this little dance-with-death with the coals, and have only a couple really swell burn scars on my arms to show for a couple decades of fire-tending, but most folks find that the wood stove gives the occasional excitement they're *really* not ready for.

Feeding the pellet stove is just boring in comparison. Firstly, the hopper door is barely warm, so no gloves required. Second, the pellet hopper is NOT where the fire is, so nothing burning can possibly escape. No gauntlets, pokers or suiting up like a medieval knight to feed the fire, no hot coals to pick up with your bare fingers. Feeding a pellet stove has about the same mortality rate as putting milk back in the refrigerator. Maybe even safer if your refrigerator hasn't been cleaned in a while, and it's "doing science" in the vegetable drawer.

CHIMNEYS

Chimneys are a major cause of heartache for wood-stovers, too. Creosote builds up, largely due to moisture in the firewood combining with unburned hydrocarbons from the fire. In a pellet stove, the extreme burning temperature and generous air supply for combustion ensures that very little unburned 'junk' goes up the flue, and the extremely low moisture content in pellets provides very little opportunity for chimney problems. While the chimney can't be just ignored completely in a pellet installation, there is far less concern of chimney issues arising. Although chimneys should still be inspected regularly, in most cases, you'll get a clean bill of health unless something really unexpected is up with your pellet stove.

FAMILY MEMBERS

As with wood stoves and any type of room heating appliance, you absolutely MUST childproof your stove if you have kids around the house, or even just visiting. Putting a metal fire screen around the stove is an excellent precaution, since crawlers and toddlers love to look at fire but might not understand second-and-third degree burns yet. I'm nursing a second-degree burn on my arm right now—cooking related, not my pellet stove—and I don't recommend getting yourself one of them, whatever their cause. Pellet stoves tend not to get very hot on the outside except for the firebox viewing glass, but keeping little hands away from any parts of the stove—including the controls—will keep everybody happier and safer. I believe that manufacturers of stoves should provide an easy way to secure all of the openings on a pellet stove, so that parents can easily prevent kids from opening control panels, doors, or the pellet hopper—perhaps just loops for a small padlock. I've heard from several parents who have added this safety mechanism themselves—drilling and tapping screws into the stove. They all find them very useful, which makes me wonder why, given that it would be cheap and easy for the makers to include it on every stove, this is not done as a standard. Makers? You out there? Safety is important; help us out here.

Another caution for parents is that pellets look a bit like breakfast cereal or dry cat food. They could present a choking hazard for very small kids, so it's important to pick up any stray pieces that escape when filling the stove. Pellets are made completely of wood, and are not toxic as such, but they do expand when exposed to moisture, so they're not suitable for people or critters to eat. While you may get all of the pellets from the bag into the hopper when loading the stove, there are occasional few loose pellets that get stuck to the outside of bags or in the creases in the plastic, which will make a break for it. So make it a habit to keep an eye out for any strays if you have animals or small kids that might decide that they look like play toys or food.

ROUNDUP TIME

Finally, there's the old "Stuff Happens". With my various wood stoves—I've had four or five models over the years—it was easy on several of them for the firebox door to close only partially. A bit of wood, ash buildup, or a clinker in the door, and the latch that seemed closed suddenly wasn't. Remember that big fire in the wood stove firebox, 45 pounds of wood, burning really slowly? Suddenly with an unlimited air supply? Hey, it's Party Time! Now it becomes its own private volcano, chunks of blazing coals are rolling across the kitchen floor, and you feel like a cowboy out on the range lassoing stray calves in a lightning storm! I'm convinced this is where many chimney and house fires begin, as well as the occasional heart attack or divorce.

If we look at this type of scenario with a pellet stove, what happens? Firstly, all of the properly constructed stoves have computerized controllers built in, including little micro-switches on the doors. If a door, either the pellet hopper or the firebox door, is left ajar, the computer tells the feed mechanism to stop feeding pellets, and the fan stops blowing in combustion air. Our little fistful of burning pellets never gets the chance to grow up into a nice raging fire, and just quietly goes out in a few minutes. A little smoke might escape.

Based on the storage and the operational characteristics of the pellet stove, I have to conclude it is probably overall one of the safest ways to heat a home. There are so few things that can go wrong and cause you worry and blood pressure problems that I have to sum up the pellet stove safety discussion with a single word: YAWN. While pellet stoves have better safety records than many other appliances or fittings in the home, it's a great idea, no matter what your heat source, to have smoke alarms and carbon monoxide detectors near each of your heating appliances and throughout the house.

NON-OBVIOUS STUFF

Before I was finally able to afford my pellet system, I researched the heck out of these things; my interest in biomass heat generation goes back almost 25 years to the very first, really crude corn kernel bio-fuel stoves I saw at a shop in New Hampshire. Despite having done considerable amount of study and prep work, I still encountered a few huge surprises once I finally had a working system in place. Some of these surprises were pleasant, and others just made me wonder why nobody had thought to write them down before. One of those surprises turned out to have a drastic effect on the fuel budget calculations we looked at earlier. It all started on an innocent trip downstairs...

PENGUINS IN MY BASEMENT?

As I went to my basement one day in February, there was a big shocker waiting for me. We'd had a pellet stove installed and running for only about a week, it was pretty cold outside, and I needed something from the basement. I walked down the stairs and it reminded me of when I was a kid and took that first dive into the local pond in the spring—you know, the pond where the icebergs finally melted last week? Man, it was COLD in the basement! About eight or ten degrees colder than I expected, and colder than it had ever been in the past. My basement is usually one of the warmest places in the house. My first thought was that the pellet stove was somehow to blame—and it was. Didn't need Sherlock Holmes to figure that out. As it turns out, the answer was super simple: after the pellet stove installation, the gas boiler in the basement almost never ran anymore. Even with the wood stove cranking its best, the propane had still been coming on early in the morning when I didn't

107

feed it on time and during the day while I was at work. I thought to myself, "Pretty Nifty!"—the new stove was obviously replacing expensive propane heat, with pellet heat, at about 1/3 the cost. I was feeling somewhat smug.

Thinking about it a few days later, something else occurred to me— my basement had been so nice and cozy before, but only because I was buying propane to heat it! The warmth I felt down there was due to the completely wasted heat from the furnace. When the boiler was running, and water circulating in my heating pipes, a significant portion of the heat was being conducted away by the air in the basement, and keeping it nice and toasty down there—right where I didn't need it. That heat was not contributing—at all—to the level of comfort in the living area upstairs. Perhaps 15-20% of the propane heat I was buying was just escaping, leaking out through the concrete of the basement walls and floor. Wasted. Totally. Now, with the vast majority of the home's heating needs being generated by the pellet stove—located in a living area of the house—ALL of the heat generated by the stove (less exhaust heat, a factor with any type of furnace as well) goes toward the comfort level of the living space.

MORE FLAVORS OF BTUS

So, here's another one of those subtle issues related to the budget, and the cost of pellets vs. other heat: even if the cost of a million BTUs of pellet heat was precisely the same as a million BTUs of oil heat, it would still be cheaper to heat with pellets, because more of the heat from the pellets ends up in your living space. This dramatically changes the cost calculation. Instead of thinking that you're keeping your home comfortable by replacing 100,000 BTUs of propane or oil heat with 100,000 BTUs of pellet heat, you are really keeping the same level of comfort in the house, but doing it with only maybe 80-85,000 BTUs of pellet heat. The saving is due to all of the heat you are paying for going right to where you want it, which is the part of the house you actually live in.

So, now the real cost of pellet stove heat is even lower than we thought, compared to furnace or boiler heat. In my case, instead of propane costing three times more than pellets for the same amount of heat and comfort level, it's probably closer to four times more expensive because I was buying "extra" propane to heat my basement and the great outdoors. Sort of like filling up your car, except for every five gallons you pour into the tank, you take out the nozzle and pour one gallon on the ground. Wasted. Heating the basement is like pouring that gasoline on the pavement. The numbers for oil heat follow the same pattern. Following this logic, it is clear that, if you place a pellet stove in the basement to heat your house, you'll end up wasting some heat there too. Still, even then, the waste heat won't cost nearly as much!

CALCULATIONS REVISITED

If you want to make better estimates of your actual cost savings, go back to the fuel-cost calculators I advised you to bookmark previously. As before, when you change each price, it chugs out a new "cost per million BTUs". Here's the trick: if you're heating with oil or propane, you are likely wasting 10% to 20% of the heat in your basement, and very little of that waste heat reaches your living space. So if the price of heating oil is $3.50 a gallon "off the truck", you should REALLY plug in $3.85 (figuring 10% wasted heat) or even $4.20 (20% waste) as the TRUE heating oil cost, to get the "cost of a million BTUs" actually usable in your living space. If you keep this calculation in mind, the budget savings for pellet heat are even more compelling. Again, fudging the calculation in this manner is only valid if your pellet stove will be located in your living area, instead of the basement or other non-living space.

Remember several sections ago, when I said that the heating calculators DID give an accurate picture of the costs of electric heat, but were NOT accurate for gas or oil without fudging the results? Now we understand why that is the case. It's because electricity is converted to heat in the baseboards, right in your living area, and no electric heat is lost warming up the basement. Despite being darn expensive, you have to admit that electric heat is at least pretty efficient. In general, if your heating appliance is not located in your living area, heat is being lost in generation and delivery to the area you really need it.

IS WASTE GOOD FOR YOU?

No longer "wasting" heat in your basement is generally a good thing, but you'll want to consider one or two potential problems. If you are using part of your basement as a living area, such as a home office, in-home craft business, or an in-law apartment, the residents of that space may find that they are getting pretty chilly without the furnace heat. Another potential problem (strictly for those of you with forced-hot-water furnace systems) is that if your heating water pipes run through a cold crawl space or an unheated garage and your furnace isn't running at all anymore, the heat pipes can freeze. There are a couple of remedies for this problem. Some systems can use antifreeze solution in the heat pipes as long as there are back-flow preventers that will keep the solution out of your drinking water. Heat-wrap tape on a temperature control can keep your pipes safe, too. Another solution I recently came across was an inexpensive device that connects into your furnace thermostat circuit and fires up the furnace on a schedule you choose; perhaps a few minutes every couple of hours, which is enough to keep a bit of warm water in the heat pipes.

SEAL IT, YOU'LL FEEL IT

One last bit of energy-saving advice here. This book is all about figuring the amount of heat you'll need and how a pellet stove fits into your scenario. However, the perfect complement to a pellet stove is energy conservation. Ensure that the weather-stripping and caulking on your windows and doors is in good shape. Add insulation to your attic. Get better-insulated windows. Even if you have to budget this over a period of a couple years, it's not a reason not to do it. If you can't make all the necessary changes at once, fix up a few items at a time. If you can't afford 15 new windows this year, get five this year and five more next year, until it's done. Buy a few rolls of insulation to do a quarter of your attic now and then get the rest when it's back on sale again. You'll start saving money immediately, and the comfort of your home will increase markedly with each step you take. The most important benefit of energy conservation is that your fuel cost should start dropping, whether it's oil, gas, or pellets for your new stove. Spending less on heating means that you can spend a little bit more on fun things. What's not to like?

OBSCURE DESIGN FEATURES

By now, you should have a good idea how the stoves work. You got your thermostat or temperature probe, your control panel, your hopper, yada yada yada. Yep, quite a few models have the same set of features, even if details differ slightly. But there are a couple of features on a few stoves that are VERY different implementations of the same functions, and could be of interest.

One thing that usually varies between different brands of stove is the feed assembly and burn pot, where the actual combustion takes place. Some stoves will pour the pellets in from above the burn pot—sort of a last free-fall swan dive before they are incinerated. On the other hand, "bottom feeders" push the pellets up from below into the fire zone. Both work fine, but there are some differences in the path the ash is transported to the ash bin as well as in the interior layout of the entire stove. Since there are proponents of both styles and major manufacturers on either side, I'm not convinced that either style has a major advantage over the other.

One item that is frequently found on stoves designed for multi-fuel use is the automatic burn-pot scraper. Alternative fuels such as corn may produce significant quantities of "clinkers" and deposits that can quickly foul and block the burn pot, and some stoves feature automatic mechanical scrapers or stirrers that periodically go in and break up these deposits. Probably not really important if you plan to burn only wood pellets, but something to keep in mind if you want to experiment with multi-fueling.

FINE IDEAS

Then there are "fines". These aren't the ones you get for hanging onto your library books too long. In pellet-land, "fines" refer to the loose dust you find in every bag of pellets. It's really just sawdust. Much of it comes from manufacturing, as the pellets are formed, extruded, and broken to size; and some comes from handling and transportation of the finished pellets. One measure of the quality of pellets is the amount of fines found in each bag, where smaller quantity generally indicates higher quality. The fines tend to go everywhere in your stove, and are a major reason we need to clean them out. Sort of like sand at your beach house. They can eventually clog your feed augers, gum up your igniters, and contribute to the ash you find everywhere inside. Some users in the online forums have even developed homemade systems to quickly sift or vacuum the fines out of their pellets before feeding them to the stove. If your stove seems sensitive to clogging up with fines, check out some of the ingenious gadgets they've put together to deal with the issue. My stove doesn't really complain even the few times I've gotten a bag that seems to be half sawdust, so I haven't messed with this at all.

The layout of your stove's innards plays a big part in how well it handles the fines. In a couple of designs I looked at when shopping, the feed augers took pellets from the side of the hopper, and the dealer mentioned that there was a trap for the fines that you had to clean out every couple of weeks. I suppose there are some considerations that led them to that particular design, but it sounded like a big "oops" to me. The model I eventually settled on has its feed auger at the bottom of the hopper; the hopper is funnel-shaped, and the auger tilts down to the burn pot. In this type of design, the fines really can't go anywhere except where gravity takes them—into the burn pot. They burn up just like the pellets, although they tend to blow out of the burn pot and make little "fireworks" inside the stove, and those ashes tend blow around and not to end up in the ash bin. Anyway, it's worth asking the dealer to explain how a particular model handles fines, and whether there is any extra maintenance involved. If your model requires extra work to deal with fines, check out some of the solutions for "pre-cleaning" the pellets found online.

There are various features unique to particular stoves, such as the possibility of using some stove models to augment your domestic hot water supply, or even run in conjunction with your existing oil/propane boiler. This sort of thing adds plumbing and complexity, and in many cases will not result in significant savings compared to the cost of setup. However, it may be worth considering in very specific circumstances, such as a commercial installation requiring a great deal of hot water, or for large buildings that require a lot of space heating. In most cases though, this is more of a job for a purpose-built pellet boiler or furnace system than for a pellet stove.

OUR OWN INSTALLATION

After years of research, I finally pulled the trigger and decided to replace my trusty, massive wood-burning stove with a pellet stove. So, after all this deliberation (mainly waiting to have some spare change to do it) what does my setup look like, and how well does it work?

We live in southern New Hampshire, so you can probably gauge the type of climate we get here - it gets pretty crisp during our winter, but not like Minnesota or Quebec; more severe than Connecticut or Pennsylvania. My house is built on a pretty open concept, with very good air circulation to all of the general living areas—it passes the "bacon test" with flying colors. It was built in 1989, and is equipped with probably about average insulation and fitted with decent windows and doors for that period.

Three floors and about 3200 square feet of living space; in volume the house amounts to about 25,000 cubic feet. In the kitchen end of the house, I have one of two conventional heating zones, as well as the pellet stove. The living/dining room, and the second conventional heating zone, is in the other end of the house. Running the system, we completely turned off the thermostat in the kitchen zone, where the pellet stove lives. It's never, ever needed. I maintain the other zone with the thermostat on a "backup" setting, in case it gets chilly in there. Still, in a couple of winters with the pellet stove in operation, zone two has only turned itself on a handful of times, and mostly because I had the pellet stove set at too low a temperature or let it run out of pellets. Oops. Operator Error.

With the pellet stove, the comfort level in the house is at an all-time high; not just in the winter, but especially in the fall and spring, when I hated popping on the furnace, but don't feel bad at all about running the pellet stove. Prior to this, we often had the conventional zone running in the living room with the attendant cold-warm-cold-warm cycle. To counter this swing, we had to set the thermostat excessively high, to avoid the chills that we would typically experience at the low point. Now, even with the actual temperature set lower, it's absolutely steady all over the house. Rooms far away from the pellet stove are a couple degrees cooler, but the steadiness of the temperature in each room makes them all feel great. It is SO nice in here now.

The two upper floors maintain a pleasant temperature, and are even occasionally too warm, although there is no heat source up there, just the heat coming up from the stove. The basement remains chilly (Yay!), because the furnace mostly only runs to provide domestic hot water. In short, except for possibly two or three savagely cold and windy days a year, the pellet stove supplies all of my heat.

The cost saving over the last two winters has been astonishing. Even though I was using one of the largest wood stoves on the market, I was not always around to feed it; either being at work during the day, or not being eager to get up a couple times in the middle of every night. Consequently, the propane bills I used to get were pretty outrageous. With the new stove, conventional heat usage drops to almost nothing. My total heat bill has dropped by $2000 or more per year, even though I had been burning several cords of wood a year. While firewood and pellets are often deemed being close in terms of cost-per-BTU, you can get some very significant savings due to the pellet stove keeping itself going without human intervention. If I'd been able to train my cat to feed the wood stove while I was at work and at night, I might never have gotten the pellet stove, but reality being what it is, my heat bill is significantly reduced, and our comfort level has markedly improved.

THE ENVELOPE, PLEASE

So, you are likely wondering what model of monster flame-throwing 2.5 million BTU dragon has tamed my savage house?

Actually, the stove model I finally bought was a US-made Harman "XXV" twenty-fifth anniversary unit, with a manufacturer's rating of 50,000 BTUs/hour. I had really wanted a different stove, mainly because I figured with a 3200+ sq. ft. house, something bigger wouldn't hurt at all; and I didn't know of any way of accurately estimating the capacity that would serve the house. My old wood stove had around a 60,000 BTU rating, and it did quite well when I got it really cranking, with the caveats of being around to feed it all day and night.

The dealer had a great deal on a different brand floor model with a 58,000 BTU rating, higher than the XXV. However, another family member objected extremely vigorously to the styling of the 58,000 model - Ugh Lee! - hey, I thought it looked nice - and we got the XXV instead. Although I was impressed with the design, features, and appearance of the XXV, I was really kind of bummed to have to "settle" for the XXV because of its smaller capacity, and I was really concerned that it would turn out to be too small for our needs. Duh. Makes me wish I'd written this book BEFORE I got the pellet stove, so I could've read it. Then reality came, the stove was installed, and we put the XXV through its paces. It really snapped MY head around! The XXV has replaced close to 95% of our propane space-heating usage.

It is definitely not too small for what we need. I expect it would do a great job heating a home even a bit larger than this one. And the comfort level is amazing.

A large part of the reason I decided to author this guide was that the experience of owning the stove has really been quite different than I had expected, even after years of study on the subject. I admit to being quite pleased with most of the "surprises", but I felt that other people interested in the subject might appreciate having some of the surprises explained BEFORE they shelled out four or five thousand bucks to switch to this type of heating.

As I said, decor was certainly a part of the decision process for us. The XXV is a sort of older, traditional style, and our home is definitely more Flintstones than Jetsons overall. Some models we saw seemed to be great stoves, but would look out-of-place here. They would fit well in a more modern style of home. We'd probably have gotten used to one of them over time, but we're really glad we settled on this model. Some of you will likely take a look at the XXV that we like so much, and decide it's just plain old-fashioned. In that case there are plenty of other models that will look just dandy in your home!

On balance, I have to admit to being deliriously happy with the Harmon XXV. It's been 100% reliable for three winters now, although some folks contributing to online forums have suggested that the igniters on this particular model burn out a bit too frequently. Apparently, Harman thought so too, and changed to a more durable design at one point. I'm actually not sure which one my stove has, since the switch was about the time we got our stove. Runs all brands of pellets that I've been able to find without any complaint, and cleans up pretty easily. The "comfort season" in our house now runs 12 months a year.

I would've also liked the option of an extended capacity hopper, for when we take off for a weekend. The XXV is noted for being a bit more hassle to clean than some other Harman models, but it's not all that bad; routine maintenance things are mostly right out front, but it has just a few more nooks and crannies than I'd like. I'm still undecided between running in room temperature mode (with the sensor), or the stove temperature mode that many recommend. I've switched to lighting the stove with the igniter, and then switching to manual mode, due to possible concerns with igniter life that I mentioned above. I purchased a battery charger/backup/inverter system sold by Harman, but haven't needed it as yet, so can't comment on how well that works.

Since my woodstove is gone, I decided to make another change – I upgraded my living room fireplace to have one of the tubular air-convection grates that direct more of the heat into the room, because that's now my only "totally power-less" backup heat system. Not a complete heat system, but at least I can keep the house warm for a few days. I'm still tweaking settings on the stove, and have tried a dozen or more brands of pellets just to see what works best, but I'd say my installation is a more or less a complete success. I'm actually even more pleased with the stove than I thought I could be, and the XXV turned out to be a near perfect choice for my household.

The XXV works great for us, but I have no financial incentive to sell you one. I'm not an employee of Harman Stoves, or of anyone in the pellet stove industry. There are many great stoves out there, and the XXV is only one of them. Harman makes a complete line of stoves of all capacities, which are considered top tier in quality and performance, but stoves by other manufacturers have received excellent reviews as well, including models from QuadraFire, Lopi, Breckwell, Englander, Enviro, St. Croix, and a dozen more.

A good local dealer that has a couple of quality lines of stoves and will service and stand behind their product is probably as important as the actual brand you purchase. Again, the online community is a super source to consider before making the plunge, as there are likely to be a dozen owners of any stove model that is on the market today, somewhere in the membership. They probably have opinions about the local dealers, too. Don't be dissuaded from a particular model, or dealer, if there are a couple of bad reports online. As with cars, every manufacturer seems to send out a lemon from time to time. However, do pay attention when someone complains about specific features that are poorly designed, for example someone might write: "the pellet feed opening on model ZZZ is too small and I spill pellets all the time". Try to compare the feature in question against other models and makes of stove and evaluate for yourself whether this might create a problem for you. Make note if particular stove models or dealers have many bad reports – that probably isn't a good sign! Finally, don't go too crazy agonizing about slightly different features of "model A" vs. "model B". True, it's a decision you'll have to live with for some years, but in all likelihood, you'll adapt to the differences, and either will do the job just fine.

OTHER PELLET APPLIANCES

While this guide mainly aims to explain what to expect from a freestanding pellet stove, I'd be remiss in not mentioning a couple of other pellet-powered heat sources.

INSERTS

First, there's a "pellet fireplace insert". These are usually placed in an existing traditional open fireplace. As you probably know, open fireplaces are fairly inefficient, and often suck more warm room air up the chimney than they replace. Inserts remedy this problem, as they allow a fireplace—which is primarily decorative—to become a major heat source for the home.

PELLET INSERT IN FIELDSTONE FIREPLACE

The insert sits inside the existing fireplace opening, and uses the existing chimney as its exhaust flue. It must be fitted properly to seal the chimney, and you should get advice and a home visit from an expert installer before committing to buying one. In my home, it seems that a pellet insert in my fireplace would be darn near impossible, because of a non-standard set of smoke baffles in the chimney. However, most chimneys can be adapted without too much fuss.

If your installation is workable, you can expect an insert to function pretty much like a freestanding pellet stove, so that much of the information in this document applies. The real major differences are that their pellet hopper volume and heat output capacities may be smaller than you would get with a freestanding pellet stove because they have to fit into a restricted space, and cleaning can be more difficult. Some inserts have rails or rollers that allow you to bring the machine out into the room a foot or two, which gives access that is a lot more convenient. Inserts are an excellent option for homes that just don't have a place for a freestanding stove, or as a second pellet heat source for homes that are too spread out or segmented to be heated by a single stove. A number of participants in the online forums have indicated that an insert fulfills most, or even all, of their home heating requirements.

PELLET BOILERS AND FURNACES

Second, there are pellet boiler and furnace systems available. These are becoming more sophisticated all the time, and can be just about drop-in replacements for an existing gas or oil furnace/boiler. They use the existing forced-hot-water heat distribution (there are also forced-hot-air versions) and—rather than from individual bags of pellets—are usually fed from a bulk pellet bin holding 5 or even 10+ tons inside or outside the house. They have auger or vacuum-driven systems that feed pellets automatically out of the storage bin, and you can leave them unattended for days and weeks at a time. A couple of things to note here are that the operational characteristics of these systems are usually similar to those of conventional heating. As a result, most are regulated with a thermostat, rather than the super comfortable heat sensor technology you find on most freestanding pellet stoves. In addition, you will probably find that you are warming your basement again, albeit with pellets this time. Still an excellent way to save on your heating bill. Many commercial stores and government buildings in our region are converting to use pellets as their primary or auxiliary heat source, and I was pleased to find that some of these larger furnace and boiler systems even incorporate variable-output features to increase temperature stability, comfort, and efficiency.

ODDS AND ENDS

Last, there are a number of "novelty" appliances. While these are not intended for home-heating as such, Amazon and other websites sell pellet barbecue grills, meat smokers, ice-fishing heaters, and a half-dozen other odds and ends that make use of pellets. I'm guessing New York City hot-dog carts will soon be using them, maybe with sauerkraut-flavored pellets? I have no idea how well any of these things work, but they might be fantastic, and you've already got a stack of pellets handy (or will have, soon). Some vendors offer pellets made from apple, mesquite, and hickory for barbecuing and smoking. I'm kind of thinking about the smoker for meat and fish myself, it seems like something where the controlled feed and heat of a pellet unit would be beneficial, especially since everything I try to smoke gently ends up black and charcoal-y on a regular grill.

Another item that I want when I win the lottery is the "snow dragon melter" for my driveway. Some cities use these to melt the truckloads of snow they plow off the streets each hour, but current ones are powered by gas or oil. They'd be awesome powered with pellets, especially since the SMALLEST-sized ones are rated over 5 million BTUs per hour – 100 times the capacity of most pellet stoves - which requires burning hundreds of gallons of oil or more each hour. They'd save a double fistful of bucks burning pellets instead. Many great applications for wood pellet heat will be on the market in the coming years.

There are many ways to get further information about any aspect of pellet stoves and their operation. Firstly, many dealers are very knowledgeable about their products and are willing to help if you have problems or concerns. Most reputable stove manufacturers have websites that provide a good deal of information and some even have online manuals or 800-number help lines. Asking friends who have pellet installations of their own is always good, as they can give you valuable information on the reliability of local dealers.

Another place that I consider a primary resource of information on "all things pellet" are the numerous web forums on the subject. While this booklet is based primarily on my own research, observations and deductions—combined with lots of hours of heckling stove dealers and pouring over sales literature, websites and manuals—I'd be remiss in not giving credit to the hundreds of members of the online wood and pellet-heat forum at "hearth.com". They've provided insight on particular stove features and quirks, innovative usage, and general all-around helpful discussion on nearly any aspect of pellet stoves that might interest you. Hearth.com is also a great resource for wood stove owners. Thanks, folks!

In particular, if you are in the market for a stove, looking for dealers, trouble-shooting problems with your stove or installation, or need recommendations on pellet performance, I would recommend browsing the archives at hearth.com . I am sure that you will find that your time is well spent. In addition, they often have used stoves and accessories for sale. That can be a great way to get a stove at a price friendlier to the budget.

WHEN THINGS GO WRONG

AW, NOW WHAT?

Okay, well, by this time if you've been drinking enough of the Kool-Aid, you'll be kind of humming the "Pellet Stove Club" theme song—P-E-L-L-E-T S-T-O-V-E (hey, fits to the tune of "Mickey Mouse"). But, there is in fact one nagging problem you'll eventually encounter when you've gone whole-hog with the pellet program.

Probably the biggest thing that's going to make you question why you chose a pellet stove is a Massive Sustained Power Outage. In much of New England recently, we've had ice storms, early season snow storms, and all sorts of unpleasant weather. These weather events can cause those fine folks at your electric utility to send you a monthly bill for $1.68, because they couldn't deliver any electricity to your home for a couple weeks. And yes, being out of power means your pellet stove is not running, too. Bags of wood pellets without a pellet stove are like a pair of running shoes without a marathon.

How do we balance wanting to have pellet heat, with the fact that it's dependent on having at least some power available? The first trick is the most appealing: become a Famous Movie Star, and take the jet down to Cancun 'til the electricity comes back! Probably not practical for all of us, though. Actually, there are a couple of feasible ways to power pellet appliances when the grid has given up.

This one's more pragmatic, and obvious to those who have been living in New England since 2009 or so—Get Y'Self A Generator. One great thing about pellet stoves is that they heat up the house very quickly. Turn it on to maximum blast, and in about ten minutes, there's going to be substantial heat pouring out, and it won't shut down while your home is warming like a boiler. You don't have to run your generator 24 hours a day. Several two or three-hour sessions a day with the generator on will likely be all you need to keep the house at least bearable and pipes thawed until the power returns.

Generators can range from whole-house automated built-in models that switch on automatically when the power quits, to portable units for working on a construction site. The prices range from $10,000 or more for some whole house units, down to a few hundred for the small job-site types. All of the large ones, and almost all of the small ones, provide more than enough power to run your pellet stove and another appliance or two. Check the wattage ratings of your stove, lights, refrigerator, phone charger, and so on to determine if you can run them all at once, or if you need to alternate between them, powering a couple at a time. Especially when running from a small generator, it's a great idea to run anything you plug in through a good quality surge protector, as the power generated is often spiky and variable, which can harm valuable electronics, including the computer in your pellet stove.

Some folks have reported success with running a stove off a DC inverter connected to your car via the cigarette lighter plug. If you need to try this, ensure that the inverter you have produces enough wattage to handle driving the stove. Since the biggest power demand is when a pellet stove is running the igniter, it's a good time to run your stove on the "manual ignition" setting, where you can light the pellets with a fire-starting cube instead of the electric igniter. Check the specifications on your stove to see if they tell what the peak and average power draw is, and ensure that, if you use an inverter, it can handle at least that much draw. My stove takes around 150 Watts while running normally, but while running the igniter, can take up to 375 Watts for a few minutes. My inverter only puts out about 200 Watts, so I'd be wise to light my stove manually and not try to use the automatic igniter.

Finally, any stove can utilize a backup battery system. At least a few brands of stove will run internally on 12 V, such as a regular lead-acid battery for quite a few hours, with a simple emergency power kit from the stove maker that is essentially a set of jumper cables.

Other brands require 110 V power, and there are kits available that will charge a lead-acid battery while the wall current is on, and switch automatically over to the battery and inverter if the power dies. A typical rating for this type of system states that it will keep your stove running for 8-18 hours, although if you run your stove for just a few hours at a time, you can stretch the battery life out to a couple of days. Beyond that, you may have to lug your battery over to a friend's house that still has power for a stint on the battery charger. Keep in mind that this kind of service is rough on battery life, and if you go this route, you should get a heavy-duty, deep-cycle type, such as a marine battery that's designed for this sort of use/abuse. Regular car batteries are designed for the constant light discharge-recharge cycle of normal automobile use, and won't pull too many cycles of discharge-only, recharge-only before they cry 'Uncle!'

Finally, a few manufacturers now offer built-in battery backup as an option on their stoves, which charge automatically while on house current. While that sounds great, you may want to ask the dealer if you can remove the battery and haul it somewhere for charging, otherwise, you could be "sittin' pretty" for the first day of the outage only.

Trouble-shooting, Part 1

This is the part of trouble-shooting you may not know, but you need it. As we've seen, a pellet stove, pellets, and your exhaust system have many possible variations, and it's a dynamic system. When your stove is new, everything is tuned within a gnat's hair. What could change?

A new brand of pellets can alter the equation. Even a brand you used last year can change this year in terms of moisture and ash content, percentage of hard vs. soft woods, burn rate, and so on. If the sensors that monitor your stove's operation have fouled, the stove's computer may be making suboptimal changes to the combustion. Your temperature sensor wire can be detached; maybe the cat's been playing with it (not mentioning any names, Samantha). Lots can happen.

So, what are the clues that the stove is no longer in tune? Look for anything that may have changed. A big no-no is a significant quantity of unburned or charred pellets in the ash dump, which can indicate your feed rate is too high, or that insufficient combustion air is present. The front window smoking up rapidly can be a symptom of the same problem. Slow ignition cycle is a big hint, although I've found some types of pellets seems to ignite much more rapidly that others. Observe the color of the ash in the ash dump; if they change from a light gray to much darker, you could have incomplete combustion, although this is likely just a result of different pellet composition. A small, weak flame, or a very large and billowy flame, can all be signs of problems; if you observe a visible smoke-plume from your chimney or exhaust for more than 10 or 20 seconds when the stove is first igniting, take it as a hint. New squealing or scraping sounds, especially when the auger is feeding, suggest that the feed system needs disassembly (maybe), or just a good scrape, vacuum, and clean. The procedure for this differs greatly from model to model, so see the troubleshooting guide in your user's manual, check online, or give your dealer a jingle.

If you see any of the above, it's not necessary to panic. Panic is definitely optional at this point, and is usually unfounded anyway. If you observe any of these problems, your very first reaction should be to clean the stove. Do it really thoroughly, even if you just cleaned it a few days ago. Get out the ash vacuum, unbolt the access panels, brush off the exhaust sensors, and brush/vacuum it until it's clean enough for brain surgery. Ensure that the holes in the burn pot that supply combustion air are clean. They gunk up over time, and a combustion chamber without an air supply is not much more than a paperweight, and a dirty and sooty one at that. Check the owner's manual for other things you can check and other trouble-shooting hints. The pellet feed rate may require a slight adjustment from one brand of pellet (or season) to the next.

Wacky air pressure can affect your stove too. If the flame is bright and hot sometimes, but sluggish and smoky at others, your house may be a little bit too airtight. Try opening a window near the stove a couple of inches and see if the flame changes for better, or worse. This can indicate that the stove is fighting against negative indoor air pressure vs. the outside. You may be a candidate for an Outside Air Kit (OAK), although their use is somewhat controversial.

Even try picking up four or five bags of a different brand of pellets, to see if they make a difference. Each pellet manufacturers' product tends to vary to some degree in quality from year to year; where last year's (and NEXT year's) pellets from Fred's Pellet Co. may be just great, this year's were made from a batch of saguaro cactus that they got a great deal on. Not to worry, I've never heard of pellets that won't burn at all, but some are better left for spring and fall. In that case, save them and get some really ferocious burners for winter.

Once you've cleaned things and tweaked everything, sit back for a couple days and see if what you've done sorted out the problem. Ashes lighter, flame brighter? Cool, looks like you're golden. No? Move on to Part 2.

TROUBLE-SHOOTING, PART 2

Stuff goes wrong sometimes. Consider your car. If you've got a long commute, or kids to take to school, you'll be driving 1-3 hours a day, 5 days a week, maybe 15 hours total. Consider your heat source. In winter, it's likely running 24 hours a day without a break for months at a stretch, including weekends. Fortunately, pellet stoves are pretty simple, and have many fewer moving parts than cars, or the stoves would be breaking down every two weeks with a 24/7 duty cycle. My regular propane boiler, in fact, has its own calendar, and knows just how to break down on holiday weekends, so I'm very pleased with the simplicity of the pellet stove; and the pellet stove has already beaten the "average time between breakdowns" of the propane boiler by a large margin. Pellet stoves are very reliable, but eventually, something is going to give that isn't just a matter of a thorough cleaning.

If you're handy, spend some time with the user's manual and online help, testing things out on the stove. A simple volt/ohmmeter can let you know if your igniter has given up. Replacing it yourself is an option, and you can likely sort it out with a few modest hand tools, saving you the cost of a dealer visit. Many of the systems on a pellet stove are fairly simple and can be examined by removing a panel or two; even if you aren't up for replacing things yourself, being able to tell the dealer what parts seem to be busted can save a second trip and additional delay.

Here's where having a reliable, local dealer is so nice. You're likely to get service in a day or three, rather than a week or five. They're more likely to have the parts in stock or quickly available. A week or six back with Mother Oil, and you'll have burned up another 300-1000 dollars in excess heating cost.

Even now, you may be able to get the stove limping along until service comes. Unless something really vital—such as the feed auger motor or combustion fan—is dead, there may be alternatives you can explore. If the igniter has given up, you can switch to manual ignition mode. If the room temperature sensor has quit, switch to stove temperature mode. Familiarity with the stove's operating modes and controls can save the day here. Give the manual a browse while waiting for the repair guys; it may save you running the regular furnace or boiler for a couple days. As with a car, there are possible solutions for when your machine is just "running rough" and hasn't conked out completely.

This is one area where a pellet stove has an advantage over a conventional heating system; the conventional system typically has no "backup modes." If the furnace fails to run, there's no second chance or limping along until whatever is broken gets repaired. I've had extensive experience with my gas boiler, and when any one of its parts or sensors breaks, it instantly and irreversibly becomes an expensive paperweight. Familiarize yourself with how the pellet stove runs, and you may be able to keep it limping along until the dealer gets your new part.

Final Thoughts

There's a lot to consider before plunging into pellet-land. I hope that this has helped, not so much with snappy answers, but with understanding how you can figure out your own answers for your own particular situation. Here's a quick reminder of some of the topics you should keep an eye on. It's hard to keep all of this in mind at once, so if you have any questions go back and skim through the relevant chapters again.

Budget is a big issue for most folks, and thinking of switching your home to pellet heat is a decision that will keep you up nights wondering if you can afford it or if you'll save anything over the long run. Go back through the budget chapters again, run your own figures. In almost every case, the answer turns out to be that pellet heat is the least expensive method you can use for heating your home, by a huge margin. Current wood stove owners should pay special attention to the budget discussions, as the economies of pellet heat vs. firewood are not straightforward. The bottom line - if you have any serious winter heating requirements, a pellet stove will save you money and likely pay for itself in just a few years.

For those who currently heat with wood, keep in mind that a pellet stove will not only save you money – even if you harvest your own wood for "free" – but is far less physically demanding to keep up with. It's a good thing if you a getting a bit older (like the author) – better economy and less effort.

The comfort of your home is important, too. Remember that the heat-output controls on modern pellet stoves are the only controls – on any type of home heating system – designed in the last 130 years.

Your conventional system? Alexander Graham Bell era. Your pellet stove? The iPhone. Pellet stoves utilize the power of computers to adjust the heat output to what's needed, when it's needed, year 'round, and can even make those shoulder-season months a lot more livable. Other conventional heating systems could, and should, eventually catch up to the technology embedded in pellet stoves, but you can get it today! Your home's heating system can join the 21st century if you want it to.

Pellet fuel itself is basically inert, as well as being immobile and non-toxic. It's safe to use, keep, transport, and anything else. That makes it about as safe as any fuel on the planet. Propane or gas leaks are potentially explosive or suffocating; oil leaks can catch fire, roll down into the river and kill all the fish, or soak into your basement floors and leave your house smelling like a refinery. Wood heat leaves you vulnerable to a cascade of hot coals whenever you open the stove to feed it. Pellets are WICKED boring. If you spill some, quickly crack out a glass of wine and sit down. They're not going anywhere. Sweep them up at your leisure.

Your community will benefit from pellet stove use as well. Many of the dollars spent on pellet fuel will stay close to the community and surrounding area instead of sending them overseas. Pay your friends and neighbors to support your heating habit. Pellets are produced sustainably, and the high-efficiency burning produces very low levels of air pollutants. Wood pellets produce far lower levels of smog-forming pollutants than burning wood in a fireplace or wood stove. On a larger scale, since pellets "grow back" over time, they are close to being carbon neutral, and a few large-scale studies have indicated they may even be "carbon negative", since high-efficiency burning releases a mix of greenhouse gases that is much less potent than just allowing wood to decay.

If you are thinking of getting a pellet stove for your home, you should remember to evaluate pragmatically your personal situation. Is your home suitable for pellet heat? The physical layout of the house is very important with regard to the portion of your home that the stove will be able to heat. The insulation and air-tightness of the home will be factors. You need to consider the interaction of a new stove with your existing heating system - whether they will COMPLEMENT or COMPLICATE each other! Think about backup heat when the power fails. Storage of the pellets themselves is vital; they must be safe from the weather, and in a location that's convenient and won't create hazards for you.

Consider children or elderly in the home, and ensure they'll be safe with a pellet-burning appliance around. Your personal physical stamina is crucial as well, as you or somebody will be hauling bags or a couple buckets of pellets to the stove daily, and performing weekly maintenance chores. I've mentioned a number of ideas to help you create solutions for each of these problems, but do take a realistic look at what the stove will mean before committing to owning one.

Pellet stove technology has matured at a phenomenal rate. When I first became aware of it more than 25 years ago, it was really just a novelty, but has now evolved into a great option for heating homes and small businesses. Acquiring his type of heat will be a giant step forward for many of you on numerous levels. The comfort and economy of heating with pellets is extraordinary. In addition, you are boosting your area's economy, and reducing the country's dependence on foreign fuels. A strong alternative energy economy based on locally sourced fuels and energy sources will be a decisive factor in our national energy future, since the global players with the most resources will be calling the tune in the years to come.

Pellet stoves can help make a future that's better for us all. Using renewable energy will move us a huge step in creating a sustainable future for ourselves, our children, and grandchildren, as well as helping the economy in your area. It's not for everyone, but if your situation is right, join your friends and neighbors who enjoy the finest heating systems on the planet.

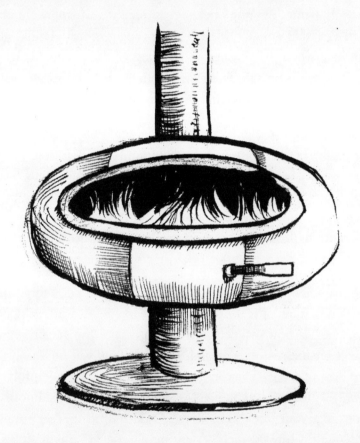

APPENDIX: RESOURCES

There are hundreds of resources, including consumer forums, environmental assessments, and stove and wood pellet manufacturers' websites, which I studied to make sense of this topic. These are some resources that were particularly helpful, but there are many more out there that contributed, as well. THANK YOU to all of those who helped in some way to make this guide possible. Here are some of them.

WEB FORUMS AND DISCUSSION

One note; when using any forum, please be courteous and search for an existing topic before starting your own; if you need to ask a question, be specific – "What's the best stove out there" questions just waste everyone's time. Instead, a question like "Would a Brand Z 'Super 12' stove be adequate to heat a 3 bedroom ranch house in central Connecticut" would likely draw useful responses from folks in Connecticut and Brand Z owners.

Hearth.com is currently the largest online forum for wood stove, pellet stove, and general wood heat topics.

www.hearth.com

Reviews from users of numerous models of stoves.

www.wiseheat.com

PELLET STOVE MANUFACTURERS

These manufacturers produce a huge range of stoves in styles from way-past-nuts modern to pre-Civil War traditional, with a wide breadth of heat capacities. You'll find something you like here. Most of these companies also manufacture wood and gas-burning stoves. There are many other companies that are not mentioned here, that are building innovative designs in stoves as well. The market is changing rapidly, and you should not necessarily limit yourself to considering the makers that are listed here.

Harman pellet stoves.

www.harmanstoves.com

Thelin Hearth Products.

www.thelinco.com

QuadraFire stoves.

www.quadrafire.com

Breckwell stoves.

www.breckwell.com

Enviro stoves.

www.enviro.com

St. Croix Stoves

www.stcroixstoves.com

Buffalo stoves.

www.buffalopelletstoves.com

England's stove works.

www.englanderstoves.com

WOOD PELLET MANUFACTURERS

Here are some of the larger pellet manufacturers that supply multi-state areas. There are likely smaller companies in your area that also produce quality pellets. Inquire with your local dealer. I found literally hundreds of pellet manufacturer listings; these are just a few of the best known ones.

New England Wood Pellet - New England

http://pelletheat.com/

Energex Wood Pellets - Canada, Mid-Atlantic

http://www.energex.com

Lignetics Wood Pellets - Idaho/Northwest, Mid-Atlantic

http://www.lignetics.com

Greene Team Pellets - Pennsylvania, Mid-Atlantic

http://www.greeneteampellets.com

Maine Woods Pellets - New England

http://www.mainewoodspelletco.com

INTERNET PELLET SUPPLIERS

Here's a web-based company that supplies pellets to much of the East Coast, and other areas. They'll give you a chance to experience pellet heat when there are no local suppliers. There were other web based distributers, but most only supply smaller, regional areas. As pellet stoves become common, new companies will emerge on the Web. Give them your support!

www.woodpellets.com

In addition, most retailers that sell pellet stoves distribute pellets in bulk themselves, or arrange with local manufacturers for distribution.

HEATING CALCULATORS

Here are a couple of useful fuel-cost calculators. At the time, they both gave realistic results, and were quite easy to use. Since websites evolve, these might not be found at these precise URLs by the time you read this, but you will still be likely to find them if you start at the home page of the site, or search the web for others.

www.hearth.com/econtent/index.php/articles/fuel_cost_comparison_calculator/

www.pelletheat.org/pellets/compare-fuel-costs

MEET THE TEAM

Ken MacDonald has been a software developer specializing in the analysis of complex scientific and business data systems since the 1970's. Outside work he enjoys kayaking, playing banjo, bicycling, gourmet cooking for friends and family, snowshoeing, winter mountaineering, and travel. This is his first publication outside of the computer field. He lives in New Hampshire with his wonderful wife and an alarmingly grey cat.

Sam Guay is a recent graduate from the Maine College of Art with a BFA in illustration. She spends her spare time fortune-telling, meandering, and having tea parties with her corvid kin and beloved feline son, Doctor Meriwether.

Find us on the web: www.pellet-almanack.com.

Made in the USA
Lexington, KY
21 April 2014